The New Bull Market in Gold

The New Bull Market in Gold

$1,000 Gold and the Many Ways to Profit from It

James DiGeorgia

With contributions by
Tom McClellan, David and Eric Coffin

21st Century Investor Publishing, Inc.

Published by 21st Century Investor Publishing, Inc.
1900 Glades Road Suite 441 Boca Raton FL 33431

ISBN 0-9718048-7-7

Library of Congress Control Number: 2004100841

Printed in the United States of America.

08 07 06 05 04   5 4 3 2 1

This publication is designed to provide accurate and authoritative information in regard to the subject matter covered. It is provided with the understanding that the publisher is not engaged in rendering legal, accounting, or other professional services. If legal advice is required, the services of a competent professional person should be sought. — From a Declaration of Principles, jointly adopted by Committee of American Bar Association and Committee of Publishers and Associations

Although both the author and 21st Century Investor Publishing, Inc. believe the information, data, and contents presented are accurate, they neither represent or guarantee the accuracy and completeness nor assume any liability. It should not be assumed that the methods, techniques, or indicators presented in this book will be profitable or that they will not result in losses. Trading involves the risk of loss, as well as the potential for profit. Past performance is not a guarantee of future results.

CONTENTS

Preface

"The possession of gold has ruined fewer men than the lack of it."

— Thomas Bailey Aldrich

Who are you to write a book on gold?
Why would anyone write a book on gold in this day and age?
Isn't gold a dead investment?

I grew up in the gold market. I was only about five or six years old when I became fascinated by rare United States gold coins. I was fortunate to receive a few magnificent gold coins as a gift from my grandfather.

My fascination with coins became a compulsion, and by the time I was fourteen I was buying and selling gold coins as a dealer. I attended most of the rare coin shows, conventions, and public auctions in the 1970s in the New York and New England areas; by the age of sixteen, in 1976, I had my own office in Danbury, Connecticut.

That was the first year of Jimmy Carter's presidency and the inflationary seventies were well on their way to making the both the gold and silver markets red-hot. Under those conditions, I became a very successful rare coin and precious metals dealer. I bought and sold tens of millions of dollars in precious metals while still in high school.

I remember going to high school with $25,000 in cash in my bag, and racing down to my office after my last class at one o'clock to go to work. By the time gold peaked and silver crashed, I had made well over $1 million. It was an amazing time in my life; and the lessons I

learned during my first bull market in gold and those years of inflation were never lost on me.

From 1981 through 1991, with the gold market drifting lower
and inflationary pressures in the United States under control, I
focused my attention away from precious metals and toward the
rare coin market. I became one of the best-known dealers in the
world and bought and sold more than $100 million in rare coins. In
truth I was a market insider. I traveled the world attending auctions,
estate sales and conventions, and I established connections with a
network of dealers and traders in virtually every major FREE city
on earth.

In 1992 I decided it was time to settle down and start a family.
I met my wife in Boca Raton, Florida. We fell in love, and at about
the same time I was approached with a wonderful new opportunity
— I was asked to write and edit the world-famous *Silver & Gold
Report.* It was a natural fit. During those few years writing the
Silver & Gold Report I was a quoted in dozens of newsletters and
magazines like *Money Magazine, The New York Times, Barron's,
Los Angeles Times, Chicago Tribune, USA Today* and others. My
articles on how to buy gold, silver and rare coins were lauded and
praised. Several rotten dealers went to prison thanks to my exposés.

But in 1997, I was convinced that gold was going to be a dead
zone for investors for many years. I retired as the editor of the *Silver
& Gold Report,* I focused my attention on high-technology stocks
and founded a new publication, *21st Century Investor.*

I was 100% right! From 1997 through 2002, the gold market
was ice cold. If you jumped out of the gold market when I left as
the editor of the *Silver & Gold Report* you did the right thing. Gold
was a dead investment.

Meanwhile *21st Century Investor* managed to ride the technology bubble all the way to its highs and better yet, my newsletter
started shorting stocks, calling the beginning of the current bear
market and recession in March of 2001. Today, *21st Century
Investor* is a thriving publication with more than 10,000 subscribers

around the world; but it does NOT focus on gold or precious metals, my first loves.

I'm writing this book to make a case for gold, because there's a dramatic shift taking place within U.S. monetary policy that is going to set the gold market on fire!

The Federal Reserve has turned on the nation's printing presses in response to a string of recent events that continue to be grave threats to world's economy:

- The bursting of the technology bubble of Wall Street that brought the Nasdaq from its lofty 5,000 level to 1,500 which evaporated more than $3 trillion of investors' nest-eggs

- The September 11, 2001 terrorist attacks on the World Trade Center and the Pentagon

- The war on terrorism

- The 2001 United States' recession

- The landslide of Wall Street accounting scandals that wiped out $7 trillion of investors' savings

- The war in Afghanistan

- The war in Iraq

- The nuclear threats made by North Korea

- The worldwide SARS epidemic

- The race by Iran and Syria to possess nuclear, chemical, and biological weapons and the failure to peaceably solve the Israeli-Palestinian conflict

- The growing risk of a double-dip U.S. recession

The shift in monetary policy to deal with the impact of these events has already prompted more than one Federal Reserve governor and Chairman Greenspan to stoke the inflationary fires by publicly asserting their willingness to resort to using the printing presses. For example:

> *"The U.S. Government has a marvelous invention for fighting deflation. This device is called the printing press. With it the government can produce as many U.S. dollars as it wishes, at essentially no cost."*
>
> — *Ben S. Bernanke, Federal Reserve Governor*
> *November 2002*

These are not just empty words. From February 2001 to June 2003, the currency component of M1 (M1 consists of funds that are readily available for spending, including cash and checking accounts) grew 20.3%, so the Federal Reserve and the Treasury Department are working like mad to reflate the U.S. economy. Investors who fail to recognize this unmistakable shift in monetary policy are putting their financial security in great jeopardy.

In this book, I will explain why 1970s-type inflation is all but guaranteed by the Federal Reserve and U.S. Government's actions in response to the string of terrible events that have occurred since 2001.

Make no mistake about it: Gold is heading to $1,000 an ounce in the next few years. If you don't hedge your real estate, stock, and bond investments with some gold, you're asking for real financial trouble.

I made my first fortune during the gold market of 1975 to 1980. For more than six years I was the editor of the *Silver & Gold Report,* the only 100% independent newsletter of precious metals in the world. I'm uniquely qualified to show you how to leverage the coming inflation and bull market in gold into a fortune. I've already done it once. For me this is a dream come true! You're supposed to get only one chance at a "once in a lifetime opportunity." This is clearly an exception to that rule — *a second chance.*

The goal of this book is to make you a great deal of money — to prepare you to recognize when it's time to cash in your gold investments and position yourself for what comes next. I'll share all of my old and new strategies with you in this book.

Chapter 1
Gold: A Brief History

At the End of the Rainbow, Gold

The history of gold, and for that matter, modern civilization, began in Ancient Egypt about 6,000 years ago. Gold was so precious and prized that it was first used to primarily forge the images of more than 2,000 gods that the Egyptians worshipped. As the supply of gold increased and Egyptian civilization flourished, pharaohs, priests, and members of the royal family used gold as an adornment in celebration of their power and wealth.

All one has to do to understand the importance of gold is to examine the royal Egyptian artifacts unearthed and on display at museums around the world. Gold leafings decorated everything from furniture to jewelry of the time period. Solid gold facemasks, earrings, bracelets, and scepters were buried with their pharaohs to serve as testimony to their power and mystical connection to the gods.

By 4000 BC, Egyptian gold production had increased enough that gold became an ultimate medium of exchange. Egyptian smelters began casting small gold bars to be used as money. Gold jewelry became a common adornment for wealthy members of Egyptian society. While gold's glory can be traced to ancient Egypt, its importance was recognized universally throughout the ancient world.

The Old Testament makes more than 400 references to gold. When God told Moses to build a shrine to worship Him, God's instructions were very specific: The shrine was to be made of gold. The references to gold in the Bible forged its importance and value to the three major western religions. Muslims, Jews and Christians use gold decoration in religious ceremonies.

It was not until around 700 BC when the Lydians of Asia Minor/West Turkey developed gold coinage. This is the beginning of gold's new monetary role as a tool for commerce and trade. Once gold was used as money, its use increased dramatically. Money was needed by everyone, whereas before, this gold was primarily used by royalty, the wealthy, and the powerful. This new use for gold also increased the *search* for gold. Gold and silver became the money of the major countries and empires throughout the following centuries.

Golden Opportunity

The supply of gold increased dramatically in the 1800s. Gold was discovered in Brazil, Russia, California, Australia, and then South Africa in the nineteenth century. The abundant supplies of gold led to the demonetization of silver and enabled gold to become the main collateral for currencies.

More gold was mined from 1800 to 1900 than in the preceding 5,000 years. In the sixteenth century, the world's mined gold totaled roughly 750 metric tons. In the last half of the nineteenth century it grew to an astonishing 10,000 tons. Annual production rose 263% from an estimated 77 tons in 1847 to approximately 280 tons in 1852, just five years later.

The Gold Standard

The increased supply of world gold led Britain to create a formal gold standard; the UK Coinage Act was passed in 1816 to establish a gold standard. But the law did not take effect until 1821 after the Napoleonic Wars when the British Parliament restored convertibility of bank notes into gold. It took until the 1870s before the rest of Europe went on the gold standard. India and the U.S. joined the gold standard in 1900.

The rules of the old gold standard (gold coin standard) included a fixed price for gold with a gold coin forming either the whole circulation of currency within a country or circulating with notes redeemable in gold. At the international level this meant a completely free import and export of gold with all balance of payments settled in gold. Before the end of the nineteenth century almost every country in the world had changed to a gold standard.

When the world entered WWI, fifty-nine countries were on a gold or gold-exchange standard. A gold standard required that all other nations on the gold standard keep their economic house in order such as inflation, employment, and balance of payments. It also required trading partners to stay on the program.

The 1930s were known for a global recession, and most nations including the United States and Great Britain abandoned the gold standard. The U.S. stayed on the gold standard until 1933 when President Roosevelt, in an effort to provide some stability to the U.S. banking system, broke the domestic dollar's link with gold by imposing a ban on the hoarding and export of gold. This is why gold pieces struck from 1900 to 1933 have such significance, as this time period is considered the Golden Era. The Gold Reserve Act of 1934 restored the convertibility of dollar notes into gold. Private buying of gold was prohibited until 1975.

One link remained between money and gold: Even though most countries abandoned the gold standard, central banks' gold reserves were supplemented by key currencies which could be redeemed for gold. The U.S. dollar became one of the key currencies. This became known as the gold-exchange standard. Initially the reserve currencies accounted for less than ten percent of the world's monetary reserves; the rest were in gold.

In 1944 the Bretton Wood Accord made the U.S. dollar the dominant global currency. By the 1960s the global economy and trade had expanded, and gold represented approximately one-third of international liquidity; the world economies were awash in U.S. dollars. The price of gold had been pegged at $35 since 1934 and there were concerns that the U.S. could not possibly fill the demand for gold if dollars were redeemed. In August 1971 the United States declared that no countries could redeem dollars for gold, and the gold standard came to an end. Some nations such as Switzerland require their internal currency to be backed by a specified percentage in gold.

Many economists feel very uncomfortable that world currencies are not tethered to an anchor like gold. This concern is probably very valid, as currencies have come and gone since the beginning of history but gold has always prevailed as a store of value.

Since most nations have adopted a type of floating currency system, the price of gold has also been able to float. For centuries the "price" of gold rarely changed, and since 1971 when the price of gold was allowed to float it has fluctuated from its initial float-ing price of $35 to as high as $875. In the last twenty years gold has fluctuated from around $265 to $500.

Gold Record

In 1980 gold reached an historic record price of $875 intraday. There are many factors that contributed to the meteoric move: glob-al inflation, the oil disruptions in 1979, and an effort in part by ordi-nary citizens and investors seeking a safe haven for their money and protection against persistent and increasing inflation.

At that time in the United States inflation was around 12%. America's world dominance was considered to be declining, and the U.S. was losing world market share in its major industries. Fiscal and monetary policies of the seventies were deemed inept. The U.S. was losing confidence in itself and in the world.

In 1979 Paul Volker was appointed Chairman of the Federal Reserve Bank and he vowed to turn the corner on inflation. Volker was a strict monetarist and placed the country on a diet of high interest rates to reverse a decade of high inflation. The price was double-digit unemployment, plummeting bond and stock markets, and anemic economic performance. Many people thought the U.S. was on the ropes. This period in U.S. economics produced some of the worst numbers in its history in terms of economic performance, unemployment, inflation, and consumer and corporate confidence.

World events were also dark. In 1979, Iranian radicals raided the U.S. Embassy and took hostages — an ordeal that lasted 444 days. At about the same time, Russia was increasing its military presence in Yemen in the Middle East, near Bulgaria's border with Yugoslavia and near the borders of Afghanistan and Iran.

Collectively all these events took their toll on investors and the general public, and in the first few days of 1980 gold prices increased from $110 an ounce to $634. The newspapers blamed the dramatic jump in price on the public's distrust of governments and paper money. In reaction to the spike in gold prices global central banks began talking about fixing the price of gold, and the U.S. Secretary of the Treasury announced that the U.S. would not auction any more gold. These statements made by the brightest economic minds in the world added fuel to the fire and prices continued to climb. Prices hit their peak on January 21, 1980 at $850.

Gold's Historical Highlights

Here is a brief outline which depicts the highlights of gold's history. We can see its evolution from an ornament to the basis of monetary systems. The history of gold is still being recorded. We encourage you to be a part of it.

Ancient Gold

6000 BC	Ancient primitives use gold as ornaments.
4000 BC	Egyptians cast gold bars as money.
1361-1352 BC	King Tut reigned. In 1922 the famous gold face mask of the boy king was discovered.
1200 BC	Gold is discovered in Andean River in Peru. Several Peruvian civilizations produce highly skilled goldsmiths.

Gold Coin Period

700 BC	Gold coins are developed in Asia Minor, modern day Turkey.
521-485 BC	King Darius of Greece adopts gold coinage, and gold coins find their way from Europe, Asia, and Africa.
356 BC	Gold medals are introduced at the Olympics.
150 BC	Romans increase the use and exploration of gold, as it is needed for the expansion of the Roman Empire.
200 AD	The decline of the Roman Empire and the world enters the Dark Ages. Gold is hoarded.
200-1200	Gold is the focus and obsession of the Byzantine Empire.
532	Ten metric tons of gold are used by the Byzantines to build the church of Saint Sophia in Constantinople.
1095-1450	Middle Ages and crusades lead to a resurgence of gold in commerce and countries economies.
1356	The King of France, Jean le Bon, is kidnapped with other high-ranking French officials. Four million gold crowns and western France was requested as ransom. This is where the phrase, "a king's ransom" was coined. French citizens revolted because of the burden.
1492	Christopher Columbus seeks a direct route to India and the Far East to seek gold and expand trade.
1500s	The search for gold by the explorers inadvertently leads to the discovery of modern-day North America — the New World — and discoveries of gold fortunes are found in Peru and Mexico.

1600   East India Company is established in England.

1600-1625   Seventy-five percent of the East India Company's
                cargo shipped to the Far East is gold bullion.

1600-1730   Much of the New World gold finds its way to
                the Far East. Asians, Indians, and Japanese do not
                use gold for money as the West does. They see
                gold as something of value; they tend to keep
                the gold and do not exchange it for other goods.
                Gold's trip to the Far East is one way.

Gold Money Period

1717   Sir Isaac Newton, "Master of the Mint," gives the
                British gold coin, the Guinea, a mandatory value.
                Some gold historians consider this the period
                during which the U.K. gold standard starts.

1797   During the Napoleonic Wars, French soldiers
                land in Fishguard, Wales. News spreads and
                causes panic all over England. Bank of England
                suspends gold payments.

1800s   Major gold finds in California, Australia,
                Canada, and Russia. The new abundance of
                gold eventually leads to the acceptance of the
                gold standard around the world.

Gold Standard Period Begins

1816   U.K. Coinage Act. Official standard unit is
                one ounce of gold.

1870-1900   All major countries except China switch to the
                gold standard, linking all major currencies to gold.

Late 1800s   Carl Fabergé begins making his now-famous
                golden Easter eggs for the czars and their families.

1886	Gold is discovered in South Africa. South Africa has become the largest gold producer.
1913	Federal Reserve Act establishes the U.S. system of reserve banks. At least 40% of note issue must be backed by gold.
1931	U.K. abandons Gold Standard.
1933	Franklin Delano Roosevelt signs an executive order making private gold ownership illegal in the United States.
1944	Bretton Woods Conference sets the basis of postwar monetary system. The U.S. dollar is to maintain a $35 = 1 ounce gold conversion rate. All other currencies are to be fixed (adjustments made in range of a band) in relation to the U.S. dollar, establishing a Gold Exchange Standard.

Gold Exchange Standard Ends

1971	U.S. dollar convertibility to gold is suspended.
1972-1973	U.S. devalues the dollar twice, increasing the value of gold to $42.22.
1973	Most major countries adopt a floating exchange rate system.
1975	After major world governments agree to not peg the price of gold, President Gerald Ford signs an executive order which makes private gold ownership legal again in the United States.
	The International Monetary Fund abolishes the official price of gold, and the price of gold is set by free market forces.

1980	Gold reaches an historic peak of $850.
1992	Treaty on the European Union signed. The Economic and Monetary Union is also established under the treaty.
1996	World central banks begin selling gold reserves.
1998	The European Central Bank decides that fifteen percent of its initial reserves should be gold.
1999	Washington Agreement on Gold announced. Major central world banks agree to cap their gold sales at around 400 tons per year over the next five years.

As long as the human race seeks beauty, power, and wealth, and as long as there is greed and fear, gold will always be pursued, wanted and needed. The history of gold is indeed not over.

Chapter 2
Gold as an Investment

Gold has been the most reliable form of money for thousands of years. It's the foundation of literally hundreds of different monetary systems because people consider gold the ultimate form of money. But gold is much more than money; it's also a solid investment.

Gold has proven to be a solid investment for three key reasons:

1. **It's the single best hedge against inflation.** When the central bankers and politicians start running the printing presses, a person is better off with gold than any other investment.

2. **It's the best financial hedge against wars, revolutions, and economic instability**. When the stock market takes a dive, investors run to gold. When governments collapse, investors buy gold. When wars break out, the world usually turns toward gold. When terrorists strike causing chaos and disorder, the public buys gold.

3. **An investment portfolio that includes gold will be less risky and outperform a portfolio made up of pure stocks in the long run.**

In this chapter we're going to take a much closer look at all three of the reasons gold is universally recognized as such an important investment. Let's begin with…

Gold as an Inflation Hedge

When you come right down to it there are only two types of assets that one can own: real assets and financial assets.

Real assets include real estate, oil, gold, commodities (agricultural commodities, base metals), and collectibles such as art or ceramics. Financial assets include stocks, bonds and other debt instruments, money market funds, and mutual funds.

Real assets normally perform better in inflationary environments because real assets appreciate when inflation rises. Financial assets perform better when inflation and interest rates are low. Low rates force bond prices higher because as rates go lower, existing bonds become more attractive (due to their higher rates) and investors bid up those prices until they reflect the new lower interest rates.

When inflation and interest rates are low the economy normally does better; lower rates stimulate economic activity with lower borrowing costs for businesses and the consumer. Stronger economic activity normally leads to economic growth, earnings growth and wealth creation. The stronger economic activity is reflected in stock prices and more money is attracted to stocks.

While the causes of inflation are similar in most economies, let's focus on the four forces that have caused and will continue to cause inflation in the United States:

1. **Easy Money:** The U.S. Federal Reserve (the Fed) is the biggest money machine in the history of mankind. The Fed has the ability to pump money into the U.S. economy at a moment's notice. There is a strong correlation between inflation and money supply growth. Too many dollars chasing too few goods drive up the prices of those goods.

2. **Commodity Inflation:** A good example of this is the disruptions or potential disruptions in the supply of oil, such as those that took place in 1973-74, 1979, 1987 and 1990. Those disruptions in a key commodity caused some of the most severe inflation in modern U.S. history. Economists call this "cost-push inflation." A price rise in a key commodity can trigger a general price rise in many products and services.

3. **Currency Devaluation:** One of the biggest warning signs of inflation is a weakening dollar. When the dollar is weak, it causes Americans to pay more for foreign goods such as

imported oil, European and Japanese cars and electronics, etc. Let's say that the Euro and the dollar are at parity. Let's also say the U.S. dollar falls and one dollar can only buy 90 cents worth of European goods; that translates into an 11% price increase — inflation. U.S. suppliers and manufacturers would be able to raise prices as the cost of foreign goods increase, and domestic prices would be allowed to increase. Years of trade deficits have created pent-up pressure on the dollar.

Note: When the dollar is weak foreign investors are attracted to dollar-denominated gold assets. Foreign currency buys more of our rare gold coins and bullion coins.

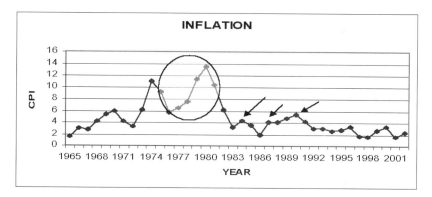

Figure 2.1: Inflation rates from 1965 to 2002

Figure 2.1 shows inflation trends since 1965. Observe the impact of inflation on gold, especially in years where inflation picks up during the 1970s, 1984, 1987, and 1990. Inflation bottomed in 2001, and after more than twenty years of falling inflation we are in the beginning stages of a prolonged period of inflation.

The Seventies and Inflation

Gold was an excellent inflation hedge in the seventies and early eighties when inflation was a global problem. Remember, this was the time period during which I made my first million investing in gold.

The seventies were known for high inflation, especially in the United States. Part of the inflation problem was inflation psychology.

Consumers and businesses buy and borrow today, because they know that in an inflationary environment borrowing costs, products, and services will be more expensive tomorrow, so increased buying activity pushes up prices even further. The cycle and psychology are very hard to reverse.

Besides inflationary psychology there were other forces that caused inflation:

- The Vietnam War: Financing a war and pursuing a full employment policy was inflationary. The Vietnam War finally ended in 1973.

- The oil embargo of 1973-1974 and 1979 created cost-push inflation. Much of the industrialized world is dependent on oil; and when the price of oil goes up so does the cost of many goods and services. For example, the airlines, transportation, chemical, leisure and utility industries' costs rise and they pass on the increased costs to the customers.

- Poor monetary and fiscal policies: For example, Nixon's anti-inflation efforts and Ford's "WIN campaign" only worsened inflationary problems.

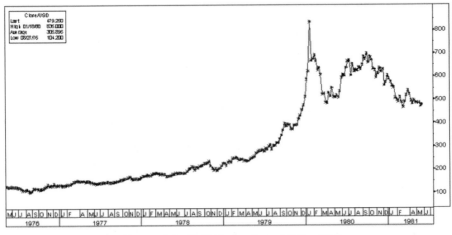

Figure 2.2: Gold Prices Late 1970s, 1980

In 1975 individuals were again able to own gold in the United States. As mentioned above, the uncertainties and spiraling inflation caused gold prices to spike to historic highs in early 1980.

1984

The United States experienced one of the worst recessions in its history in the early eighties. The Fed finally started to lower rates in 1982; fortunately, economic activity surged and we were pulled out of recession. By the first quarter of 1984 the economy was growing by approximately 10%, causing inflationary pressures. The gold market had already anticipated the rise of inflation. Throughout history gold has been a reliable anticipator of inflation. The Fed, as it did earlier, slammed on the economic brakes by sharply lifting rates which brought inflation back under control.

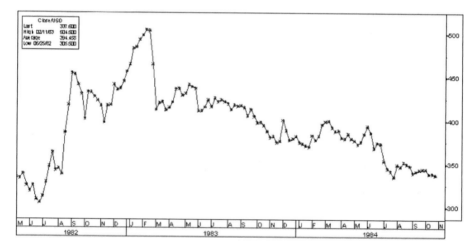

Figure 2.3: Gold Prices 1982-1984

As with most markets, the gold market is anticipatory, and it started rising in anticipation of rising inflation in 1983. The Fed started lowering rates in November of 1981 and accelerated those cuts beginning in July 1982, setting off a bull stock market and stimulating strong business activity. Inflation had dropped to 3.2% in 1983 from over 13% in 1980.

Inflation did increase to 4.4% in 1984 as anticipated by the gold market. Investors were still nervous about inflation and moved to gold, sending prices from a low of about $300 in 1982 to over $500 in 1983.

The Fed pushed up rates in 1984 to slow down the economy and slow down inflation.

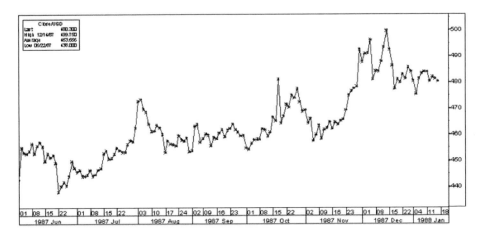

Figure 2.4: Gold Prices in 1987

The forces of rising inflation, higher interest rates, a falling dollar, and investor panic cause gold prices to jump.

Stock Market Crash of 1987

Do you remember what you were doing when the stock market crashed on Monday, October 19, 1987? On that day the Dow Jones Industrials dropped 508 points, or 22.6%. This was the largest one-day drop in stock market history. There was not any single event that caused the stock market crash of 1987. The market had been sliding for several months leading up to October.

Here are some of the reasons experts offer to explain what caused the stock market crash:

- **Valuations:** The market went from being undervalued at the start of the bull market in 1982 to historically overvalued by 1987. The Dow Jones Industrials had tripled since the start of the bull market.

- **Easy Money:** In 1985 and 1986 the Fed pumped money into the economy, then the new Federal Reserve Chairman

Greenspan took office August 11, 1987, just two weeks before the top; he immediately began raising interest rates.

- **Falling dollar:** This caused worsening trade deficits.

- **Program trading and portfolio insurance**

- **Congress considered legislation to curb takeovers:** Mergers, acquisitions, and takeovers were very popular in the eighties and were a main driving force behind higher prices; investors felt that without them the market would become less attractive.

- **Oil prices increased:** The Iran and Iraq War caused concerns about oil supply disruptions; the U.S. escorted oil tankers through the Strait of Hormuz. Oil prices started creeping up in 1987 after crashing from $30 to $11 a barrel in 1986.

- **Panic:** As the market unraveled on October 19, 1987 panic set in.

1990: Gulf War

Looking back at the Gulf War, Saddam Hussein was very bold. After invading Kuwait, he started moving his troops towards Saudi Arabia. Just imagine: If Saddam Hussein had been successful in invading Kuwait and Saudi Arabia, this madman would have controlled more than 40% of the world's oil, a very scary thought. Fortunately the world, led by the United States, would not accept that scenario, and Saddam's troops were forced out of Kuwait. The war caused a dramatic upward spike in world oil prices, inflation, and gold prices.

Inflation rose during the Gulf War period thanks to higher oil prices. We can see in Figure 2.5 that gold prices spiked when Saddam Hussein invaded Kuwait in August of 1990, when fear and worry were maximal. As the war plans began to unfold and the future began to look clearer, gold prices began to slide back down from the crisis level peak.

This teaches us an important lesson: One must buy gold before a crisis becomes evident. Waiting for dire times to arrive before buying gold is a sure way to miss the move.

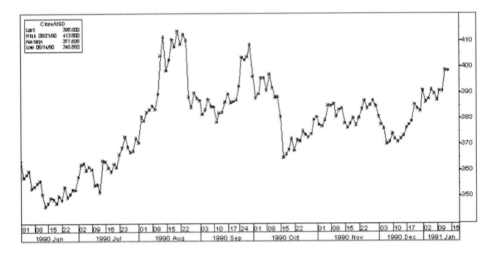

Figure 2.5: Gold Prices and the Gulf War

Gold in Uncertain and Chaotic Times

Earlier in this chapter we learned what happened to gold during inflationary times, the stock market crash of 1987, and the Gulf War. Let's look at a few more examples of what happens to gold during chaotic, uncertain times.

There are many stories in history of gold being hoarded or the price of gold jumping during chaotic and uncertain times. Here is a classic example: In 1815 when news spread that Napoleon escaped from Elba and returned to France to raise an army, the price of gold in the London market jumped from $4.66 an ounce to $5.70 per ounce in one day. When Napoleon was defeated in the Battle of Waterloo, prices moved lower.

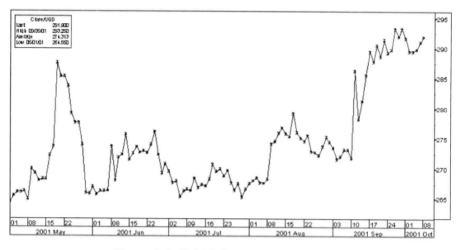

Figure 2.6: Gold Prices and September 11

The horrible events of September 11, 2001 led investors and individuals to the safety of gold. Prices advanced more than 10% immediately after September 11, then began slowly working back down to pre-attack levels. Again, if one waits for the crisis and then buys, one misses the upward movement.

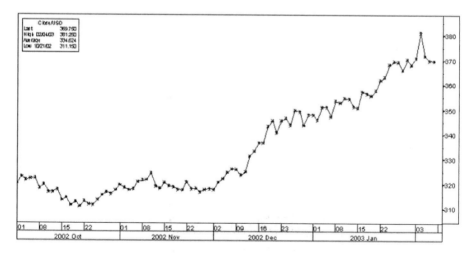

Figure 2.7: Gold Prices and the War in Iraq

As the United Nations and the United States debated the removal of Saddam Hussein and weapons of mass destruction from Iraq, gold prices rose steadily. It became clear that the U.S. was going to act on its own, which caused the price of gold to fall steadily from February to April 2003.

Gold prices do well when the potential for crisis or calamity is increasing. Once resolution starts to appear, the crisis premium comes back out of gold prices.

Gold for Diversification

Some of my best friends are very well-known financial advisors. While every one of them knows the advantages of diversification, none has recommended the inclusion of gold in their clients' portfolios – ever. That's a terrible shame; it's very shortsighted and dangerous. Anyone who has really studied value and the history of gold would immediately recognize that the importance of including gold in every investment portfolio. Don't just take my word for it...

- In 1952 Nobel Prize-winning economist Dr. Harry Markowitz introduced what is known as the Modern Portfolio Theory (MPT). One of the key tenets of MPT and efficient portfolios is the need for investors to include assets whose price movements are not correlated to each other. An efficient portfolio contains a mix of assets that can provide maximum returns with the lowest amount of risk.

  A portfolio needs to include a mix of assets that are not related. A good example is a mix of gold and stocks. When stocks are down, gold is normally up and vice versa. This type of portfolio will outperform a traditional portfolio in the long run. Owning ten different growth mutual funds is not a way to diversify since they would all tend to move together.

- In March 2003, Colin Lawrence, honorary professor with the Cass Business School in London, published a paper, *Why Gold Is Different from Other Assets? An Empirical Investigation*, and his paper confirmed the lack of correlation between gold, stocks and bonds. He concluded that an allocation of gold could help create an efficient portfolio.

Gold tends to perform extremely well in a portfolio when you really need it to. We have explained how gold performs well during inflationary and chaotic times, and how stocks perform poorly during these times. Gold and stocks together epitomize a portfolio that can reduce risk and enhance returns. Below are several graphs that exhibit difficult stock market environments and the strong performance of gold.

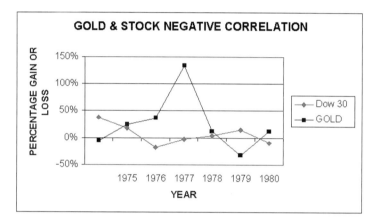

Figure 2.8: Gold Versus Stocks, 1975-1980

Figure 2.8 shows us that gold performed extremely well when the stock market was struggling, especially in the years 1976, 1977 and 1980.

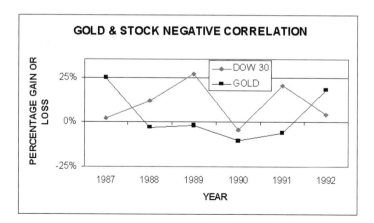

Figure 2.9: Gold Versus Stocks, 1987-1992

Here is another good example of gold's ability to perform when needed. In Figure 2.9 we can see gold's positive performance in 1987 and the early 1990s. For example, in 1987, the year of the stock market crash, gold performed extremely well. Also in 1991 and 1992 gold performed well when stocks did not.

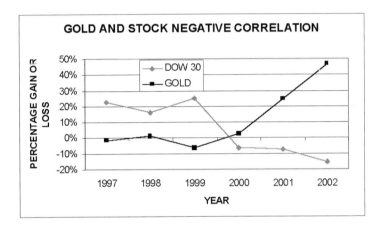

Figure 2.10: Gold Versus Stocks, 1997-2002

Again in Figure 2.10 we can see that gold performed well when investors needed it to.

Let's look at a portfolio example during this period. Portfolio A consists of 100% stock (invested in the Dow 30 Index) and portfolio B includes 70% stock and 30% gold.

The cumulative return of the Dow 30 Index portfolio during this five-year period was 7.48%. A $100,000 portfolio at the end of the five-year period would be worth $107,482.70.

Portfolio B, with 70% stocks and 30% gold would have had a cumulative return of 28.67% and would be worth $128,670.61 at the end of the five-year period, significantly better than the pure stock portfolio.

Let me summarize these important performance numbers.

Portfolio A: $100,000 invested only in stocks over five-year period would be worth **$107,482.70.**

Portfolio B: The balanced portfolio of 70% stocks, 30% gold over a five-year period would be worth **$128,670.61** (a $21,187 improvement). Gold in a portfolio can make a difference.

Buy the Rumor, Sell the News

There is a saying regarding investing that is very appropriate for gold: "Buy the rumor and sell the news." What this means for investors is that to make money one must anticipate events, not react to them. Don't wait for inflation or crisis to happen. Instead, position yourself beforehand to profit.

Figure 2.11 illustrates gold's ability as a fourteen- to fifteen-month leading indicator for inflation (consumer price index less food and energy).

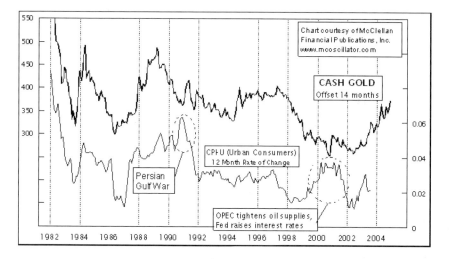

Figure 2.11: Gold prices lead to inflation

Chapter 3
Political and Global Changes

My interest in gold was cultivated in the seventies when the United States experienced an incredibly bad wave of inflation and the price of gold shot up to record highs. Every facet of our economy and political system was under siege.

The United States' economy was falling victim to a series of domestic and international events that forced the U.S. government to pursue what was then known as a "guns and butter policy." This is when a government tries to fund an expensive war while still going all out to deliver domestic social programs to its people. During the 1960s the United States underwent a social upheaval that included the inauguration of President Johnson's "great society." At the same time it funded both a virulent cold war and a shooting war in Vietnam.

The spending in Washington, as a percentage of the Gross Domestic Product, reached enormous historic levels. The spending resulted in spiraling federal debt. The U.S. government was running the printing presses around the clock at the Bureau of Engraving and Printing.

President Nixon was the first to attempt to battle inflation by ordering wage and price controls during a prime-time national address televised on all three major networks. Curtailing government spending wasn't part of his program. In fact, while Republicans often claim the mantle of fiscal responsibility, federal spending increased 95% during Nixon's six years in office.

President Ford followed with a national slogan and little pins that read, **WIN** — Whip Inflation Now. The economic woes of the United States and the rate of inflation were exacerbated by the compounding impact of Arab Oil Embargo of 1973-1974.

President Carter's attempts to get inflation under control were even worse. Inflation was 4.9% when Carter began his presidency, and by the 1980 election inflation was nearing 12%.

The wave of inflation that occurred during the Carter administration was caused by:

- Organization of the Petroleum Exporting Countries' (OPEC) dramatic increases in its price targets for oil in 1978, which reached $30 a barrel. This high price was fortified in 1979 by the Iranian revolution that sharply reduced its oil production and exports.

  President Carter responded with a feeble energy program that was based almost entirely on conservation and higher federal taxes on gasoline. President Carter addressed the nation in his cardigan sweater urging Americans to reduce their consumption of energy by lowering their thermostats at home. I lived in Connecticut at the time, and I can tell you that speech went over like a lead balloon.

- The budget deficits were close to 3% of the national Gross Domestic Product (GDP), and Carter did little to control government spending. From his first day in Washington he was battling Congress; and although it was controlled by his own party, Carter was treated like an outsider. Any attempts Carter made to reduce congressional spending were simply ignored.

- The U.S. trade balance (exports/imports) was in a deep deficit and the lack of our trading partners' confidence in President Carter led to a drastic fall in the dollar. This environment contributed to the worsening situation like kerosene to fire, making inflation much worse and leaving the cleanup to Ronald Reagan.

During the 1970s gold outperformed every other asset. Financial assets took a beating. Throughout the 1980s and 1990s inflation got under control, the U.S. dollar strengthened, gold prices dropped, and financial assets soared.

I'm convinced gold is about to reassert its dominance and rise sharply to a new high of more than $1,000 an ounce in response to a new wave of inflation that is guaranteed by a series of events that began with the September 11, 2001 terrorist attacks. Those heinous attacks have forced the United States government to once again attempt a "guns and butter" economic policy that can only result in double-digit inflation.

Already we're seeing the initial inflationary forces gathering:

- **Military Spending:** The biggest military buildup in human history, two full-fledged wars and a worldwide hunt for terrorists.

- **Homeland Security Spending:** The biggest domestic government program since Social Security.

- **Massive Tax Cuts:** $350 billion in tax cuts, etc.

- **Monetary Policy:** Using the printing presses to stave off deflation, with M3 up 20% since George W. Bush became president.

- **Oil Shock:** The biggest potential oil shock in history.

Already these factors have resulted in a major shift in supply and demand, witnessed by the rise of gold from a low of $253 in 2001 to an intraday high of $390 during the War in Iraq!

Watching this develop prompted me to personally move much of my wealth out of financial assets and into gold and rare gold coins. I'm also hedged with holdings in real estate, which perform very well in economic environments plagued by high rates of inflation.

In this chapter and the next we will show how global, political, and economic changes will dramatically increase the demand for gold and fulfill my projection of gold's rise to over $1,000 an ounce.

Policy Shift from Growth to Security

The unfortunate events of September 11 changed the world and our view of it. It will continue to have a profound effect on world politics and the economy for years to come. President George W. Bush and his administration declared war on terrorism. They said this will be a long and difficult war. We have already fought wars in the Gulf, in Afghanistan, and Iraq. Bush and his administration realize the world is a dangerous and scary place and that they must do something about terrorism, not wait to be a victim again.

I think we all look at the world differently. These events have impacted they way we travel, how we see the future, and security has become a focus for all of us. The U.S. government has certainly shifted its focus from economic matters to security.

In the next few pages I will discuss the alarming proliferation of weapons of mass destruction (WMD). Unfortunately these are the sobering realities of our time. These realities are driving new world-views and new economic and political policies.

Chemical Weapons

Chemical weapons have been used in wars for thousands of years. Sarin, VX, and mustard gas are some of the gases the world has stockpiled. These are dangerous gases that, if used as weapons, have massive deadly consequences. But the fear factor involved is just as powerful and important as the actual death toll these chemicals could cause. People fear the gruesome sort of death and suffering these chemicals can cause in the same way they fear terrorist attacks more than hurricanes. This is what makes these weapons so powerful — they not only kill; they influence the public's behavior.

Below is list of the countries purported to be capable of using chemical weapons.

Country	Chemical Weapons Possession	Comments
China	Possible	Maintains it has destroyed its stockpiles. The United States is not sure it has.
Egypt	Known	Has supplied Iraq and Syria with chemical weapons, and has used mustard gas in a past war.
India	Known	Has pledged to destroy its weapons.
Israel	Possible	Believed to be working on a program.
Iran	Possible	Began working on its program after Iraqi chemical attacks in the Iran-Iraq War during the 1980s.
Iraq	Possible	The War in Iraq was initiated to rid Iraq of any weapons of mass destruction.
North Korea	Known	Has a large stockpile.
Russia	Possible	Is destroying its stockpile.
Sudan	Possible	Has been trying to acquire chemical weapons from countries that have the capability.
Syria	Likely	Has a large and advanced program and is thought to have received weapons of mass destruction from Iraq.
United States	Still working to destroy stockpiles	Defensive research only.
Terrorist Groups	Possible	Have interests in acquiring chemical weapons.

Biological Weapons

Science has eliminated many lethal diseases such as smallpox and malaria. Science has also developed designer diseases that, if deliberately released, would be disastrous. Anthrax, Ricin and Smallpox are some of the most feared biological weapons that are being stockpiled by many countries. The following list includes countries suspected of possessing these dangerous weapons and those that are interested in acquiring them:

Country	Biological Weapons Possession	Comments
China	Possible	Claims it has never owned bio-weapons.
Egypt	Possible	Believed to have a program.
India	None	Conducts defensive bio-weapons research.
Israel	Possible	Believed to be working on a program.
Iran	Possible	Began working on program after the Iran-Iraq War.
Iraq	Possible	The War in Iraq was initiated to rid Iraq of any weapons of mass destruction.
North Korea	Possible	Believed to have a program.
Russia	Possible	Claims its bio-weapons have been destroyed.
Syria	Possible	May have a basic program.
United States	None	Defensive research only.
Terrorist Groups	Possible	Have interests in acquiring bio-weapons.

Nuclear Weapons

Nuclear weapons are the most feared weapons of all, because they are the most destructive. Even after they have exploded, they emit high levels of dangerous radiation. Nuclear weapons were new to the world in the last century; they were considered the weapons of last resort. With more countries possessing them, world leaders are concerned that they can no longer be considered the weapons of last resort. Some countries consider possession of nuclear weapons a source of national pride and achievement. Leaders are also concerned that these weapons can end up in the hands of terrorists.

Many military experts do not consider "dirty bombs" weapons of mass destruction because the damage is not as devastating as a conventional nuclear bomb. However, if a dirty bomb were used it would probably cause widespread panic, and the damage to the economy would be enormous.

Country	Nuclear Weapons Possession	Comments
China	Known	Has 400 weapons and enough material to make many more.
Egypt	None	Possesses no weapons but it does have the technology
India	Known	Has a small stockpile, but enough material to make 100-150 nuclear warheads.
Israel	Known	Possesses 100-200 bombs.
Iran	Possible	Pursuing a nuclear program.
Iraq	Possible	The War in Iraq was initiated to rid Iraq of any weapons of mass destruction.

Pakistan	Known	Believed to possess 35-50 bombs.
North Korea	Possible	Believed to possess a small number of bombs.
Russia	Known	Has approximately 5,400 warheads and at least 4,000 tactical nukes.
United States	Known	Has approximately 5,900 warheads and 1,000 tactical nukes.
Terrorist Groups	Possible	Have been seeking to acquire weapons since the 1990s. According to intelligence sources enough nuclear weapons material has left Russia to build a bomb.

Terrorism

What has most governments and citizens worried is the possibility that these weapons could get into the hands of terrorists who would not be afraid to use them. Terrorism experts say that the terrorists of today are bold, imaginative, and very motivated by their beliefs. The United States was exposed to anthrax in several communities where five people died and 22 people were infected after September 11, 2001. My business and home are located in Boca Raton, Florida — one of the affected cities — so I have learned to take these risks seriously. Many of the major cities around the world are preparing for such events. Terrorism is a daily fact of life in some parts of the world and now it is spreading.

Many experts are concerned that Al Qaeda and other terrorist groups intend to cause a major economic catastrophe in the United States. In the next section we'll examine several other scenarios that can cause an economic crisis.

Post-September 11

An exhaustive study sponsored by the Council of Foreign Relations concluded that the United States is still dangerously unprepared to prevent and respond to a major terrorist attack on U.S. soil. They also believe that we will have another attack within the next few years. The research was undertaken by a non-partisan group that includes politicians, military leaders, former high officials from the FBI and CIA, and some of the nation's legal, financial, and medical authorities.

The study brings up many concerns regarding funding, staffing, training, cooperation and coordination between domestic and international agencies. It also reports that many ships, trains, and trucks that enter the United States are not inspected, making it fairly easy for terrorists to transport weapons of mass destruction to the U.S. They also believe that our energy refining and transportation infrastructure is highly vulnerable. We discuss this issue in the next chapter, as the economic ramifications are incalculable.

Another report by the U.S. government given to the United Nations in 2003 said that there is a "high probability" that Al Qaeda will attempt an attack with a weapon of mass destruction in the next two years.

The report had other sobering statements:

- Despite recent setbacks, Al Qaeda maintains the ability to inflict significant casualties in the United States with little or no warning.

- The Al Qaeda network will remain the most immediate and serious terrorism threat facing the United States for the foreseeable future. It may seek softer targets, like malls, banks, and places of recreation and entertainment, but will also pursue attacks similar to those of September 11.

- Searches of more than forty sites in Afghanistan used by Al Qaeda yielded documents, diagrams, and material that revealed an appetite for weapons of mass destruction.

- FBI investigations have revealed an extensive widespread militant Islamic presence in the United States. Some of these militants are expected to have links to Al Qaeda, and it is expected they will be involved in future attacks.

Unrelated to the United Nations report, a recent article in a major business magazine discussed security gaps between the FDA and the two million farmers and thousands of importers, livestock feedlots, and food processors who are vulnerable to an attack. The FDA has published reports regarding terrorists' threats to our food supply, but portions of the reports are secret and can't be shared with the food industry.

Some of the dangers that the report discusses include using foot-and-mouth disease and the poisoning of processed foods or imported foods. The FDA and food industry leaders are looking for solutions regarding the security gap so the food industry can take precautions.

Post-War in Iraq

One of the major objectives of the War in Iraq was to create some stability in the Middle East and establish Iraq as a friendly democratic anchor nation, and then leverage that democracy to other parts of the Middle East. This change could also lay the groundwork for lasting peace between the Israelis and Arabs. These are big dreams. Unfortunately we are far from achieving those goals — Iran is building its nuclear capabilities, Syria has always harbored terrorists, and there are debates about whether they are hiding Iraq's weapons of mass destruction and key Iraqi leaders. Every day there is news of American soldiers' lives being lost. In the next chapter we discuss the tenuous rule of the Saudi royal families. We haven't even discussed the threats of North Korea, India, and Pakistan.

The war on terrorism is impacting the world economy. In the 1990s there was free flow of capital, innovation, and skilled and talented workers. This trend has reversed and will slow the global economy. Many economic changes and trends are developing. Our country has joined the list of many countries whose concerns have shifted from having a desire for economic growth to craving security.

Gold has a long history of maintaining its value during times of increasing world stress. Individuals and institutions will continue to seek the safety of gold, which increases the demand for gold. Another terrorist attack against the U.S. or one our allies or neighbors could easily cause the price of gold to jump to over $500. Obviously, I would not want to see this happen, but experts think it can happen, and you have to protect yourself against that possibility. Just as you would protect yourself physically, you must protect yourself financially.

Chapter 4
Economic Troubles and Bubbles

The last chapter focused on the changing global and political trends and the dangers that we face, including the experts' opinions that the United States will be attacked again on its own soil in the next few years. We have faced these dangers before, and we have recovered. If we are once again attacked, it will be very difficult to recover economically because our problems are larger and the tools we have to solve our economic problems are losing their effectiveness. We are very vulnerable to a serious financial crisis.

Gold will be a major solution to help investors through the next financial crisis. Gold has been and probably always will be the only true form of money. All one has to do is look at economic history objectively to realize that gold has been the only universally recognized store of wealth for the past 5,000 years. In times of war, revolution, economic disruptions and social and political scandals, gold has continually proven itself as the most reliable store of wealth.

The growing economic problems now facing the United States that will have a major impact on the markets and gold include:

1. Growing dependence on foreign oil and the potential for an oil shock

2. The devolution of banking and the Federal Reserve Bank

3. Proliferation of derivatives

4. U.S. budget deficits

5. Ballooning consumer, corporate, and government debt

6. Inflation

7. The falling value of the dollar

Oil Shocks and Higher Oil Prices

All the major world recessions of the last thirty years have had their roots in either disruptions in oil supplies or high oil prices. Each of the great industrial economic powers of the world is very dependent on oil. The cheapest and most abundant sources of oil come from the Middle East, an unstable and unpredictable part of the world. Investors and businesses have learned to keep their eyes on oil prices and the Middle East, specifically Saudi Arabia, the world's largest oil producer.

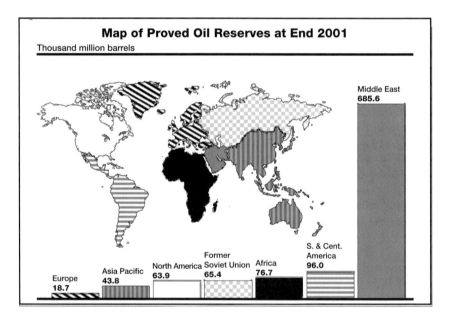

Figure 4.1: World's Proven Oil Reserves

The Middle East possesses approximately 65% of the world's oil reserves. Saudi Arabia has approximately 261 billion barrels of oil, which is about 25% of the world's oil. Having an economy which is dependent on oil leaves the world vulnerable to the fluctuations of Middle East oil production.

One of the most disturbing facts about the September 11 attacks was that fifteen of the nineteen participating terrorists were Saudis. Saudi Arabia is home to Islam's two holiest shrines, Mecca and Medina. The kingdom outlaws public worship of all religions except Islam. There have been many news articles describing the fragile rule of the royal Saudi family and the ultra Islamist religious leaders who have abundant influence in Saudi society. Islamic leaders control much of the education of Saudi citizens. Young Saudis are taught a very extreme form of Islam, and when most graduate from school they have very few opportunities. Young Saudis are ripe for recruitment for Al Qaeda and other Islamic extremist groups. Remember, Osama Bin Laden is from Saudi Arabia.

The 2003 bombings in Saudi Arabia that killed 34 and injured around 200 are linked to Al Qaeda. Al Qaeda and other Islamic terrorist groups are very interested in overthrowing the Saudi royal family and replacing it with an ultra-hard-line Islamic regime. Anti-terrorist experts report that Al Qaeda has wide support across all levels of Saudi society. Sympathizers give money, shelter, and other forms of aid. Intelligence sources warn that there will be other terrorist attacks in the Saudi kingdom including attacks on targets like the oil industry, especially pipelines that could be attacked easily and that would cause major economic disruptions around the world. Other Saudi experts report growing hard-line fundamentalism that is spreading throughout the country. These conditions in Saudi Arabia are eerily similar to events in Iran during the late 1970s, when the rise of the Revolutionary Iranian Islamic movement eventually drove the Shah of Iran into exile.

Look what happened to oil prices when the Iranian Revolution took place in 1979. The world saw an oil crisis and the U.S. saw sky-high prices and long lines at the gas pump.

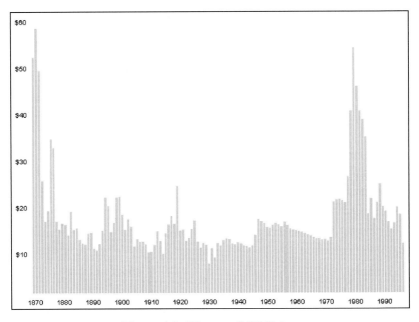

Figure 4.2: History of Oil Prices

The high oil prices of the late seventies and early eighties occurred during the Iranian revolution and the beginning of the Iran-Iraq War. The conditions in Iran in 1979 were similar to the conditions occurring in Saudi Arabia today.

Some anti-terrorism experts think that certain strategic areas in the U.S. could be prime targets for terrorist organizations. Houston is an example; it has certain attractive advantages for Al Qaeda. The city has a fairly large Middle Eastern population to provide cover for any attackers. Several airlines provide direct flights from Houston to the Middle East. The worst-case scenario would be an attack along the Houston Ship Channel where a substantial portion of the U.S.'s refinery capacity is located. The entire area of refineries would create a huge explosion resulting in a cloud over Houston that would make the metro area unlivable for a significant period of time. This is an area where 4.25 million people live and work. The economic damage would be incalculable to the U.S. and world economy.

What makes matters worse is that we are much more dependent on imported oil than we were thirty years ago.

Figure 4.3 shows the increased vulnerability of the U.S. to oil disruptions because of the high amount of imported oil from the top five oil suppliers.

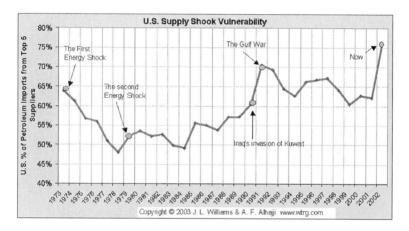

Figure 4.3: U.S. Percentage Imports for Top Five Suppliers

Figures 4.4 and 4.5 illustrate the impact higher oil prices have on the market. Investors should always pay close attention to oil prices and the Middle East.

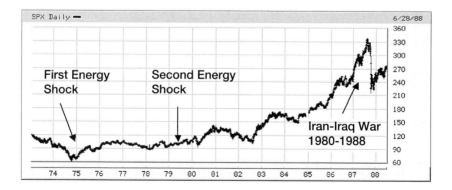

**Figure 4.4: High Oil Prices and Disruptions in
the Stock Market, S&P 500, 1973-1990**

**Figure 4.5: High Oil Prices and Disruptions
in the Stock Market, S&P 500, 1990-2003**

The Changing Role of the Federal Reserve and Banks

Congress passed the Full Employment and Balanced Growth Act in 1978 and it mandated the Federal Reserve to maintain price stability and generate conditions to create full employment. The Fed has used three tools to achieve these goals:

- Open-market operations

- Reserve requirements of member banks

- Changing key interest rates to member banks

For decades, the U.S. Federal Reserve Bank has had tremendous power over the economy. Briefly, it could expand the economy by lowering key rates and buying government securities in the market and/or reducing reserve requirements to banks that would in turn lend capital to economic areas that have the most potential. If the Fed wanted to slow down the economy, it would reverse the process by raising key rates, selling government securities in the market and raising reserve requirements.

During the downturn of every business cycle, "banking sins" are exposed. These "sins" are exposed through banks' bad lending practices such as real estate, Latin American loans, the Savings and Loan crisis, the Orange County, California bankruptcy, and long-term capital management. I call these "banking sins" because they are far beyond bad lending practices.

The biggest changes that have occurred structurally in our economy are the increased practice of securitizing loans and the proliferation of derivatives. After decades of uncovering bad loans, banks and Wall Street have decided to spread their credit risk to insurance companies, institutional investors, and ordinary investors by packaging their loans and selling them to investors. I have several friends who have been corporate bankers for years. Years ago when they started in banking, they provided loans to their corporate clients and carried those loans on the bank's books. This has changed. They now participate in syndicate packaged loans, and then they sell the loans to investors. Instead of collecting interest income, they now collect syndicate fees and other fees from bank services they can sell to the client.

Theoretically, this sounds good. Loans are spread out among many investors and the banking system is healthier and safer. Bankers and Wall Street point to the recent tech and telecom bubble to prove the supposed advantages of these schemes. Big banks and Wall Street maintain that if all the technology and telecom loans that were made in the nineties and the bankruptcies of WorldCom, Adelphia, and Global Crossing had been on the banks' books, then we would have had severe problems in the banking system. U.S. banks are healthier in this recession than during past recessions, but there are many problems that can occur with these new changes:

1. Fed losing control of economy to the capital markets

2. Loans not based on creditworthiness but on loans' marketability

3. Improper allocation of capital

4. Borrowing short-term to lend long-term

5. Few understand all the derivatives that are being created

6. Credit booms lead to asset bubbles

It is becoming increasingly difficult for the Fed to achieve its mandate of full employment and price stability with traditional tools. The Fed has dramatically pumped money into the economy since 1995 to avoid economic problems caused by the collapse of the Thai baht and ensuing Asian contagion, the default by Russia on its debt, the Long-Term Capital Management crisis, and potential problems with Y2K. The downside to keeping our economy going by increasing the money supply was the creation of asset bubbles, especially in the technology and telecom sectors in the economy and the stock market. The Fed's tools of lowering rates and pumping money into the economy has not worked effectively in the early 2000s — interest rates are close to zero, the economy is stalled, unemployment is rising and potential bubbles are occurring in the bond and real estate markets. If we have another crisis, the Fed will not be able to lower rates to keep the economy going.

I have presented the potential problems caused by oil crises and terrorist threats, but I also want to discuss another problem that has plagued our markets and the economy in the past and could plague us in the future: derivatives.

Derivatives

Derivatives are comprised of a very broad category of assets which include convertible bonds, options, futures, and forward contracts. Derivative values are based on the performance of an underlying asset. Derivatives are used by hedge funds, institutions, companies, speculators, and individuals. This area of investing can be very complex, but I will be brief. I will highlight past problems derivatives have posed to our markets and the economy. Warren Buffett, in his 2002 annual report, warned of the potential problems our economy faces with derivatives. He speaks from his experience operating a reinsurance company that Berkshire-Hathaway bought and the problems that company has faced with derivatives.

Briefly, the problems with derivatives that have appeared in the past that may crop up in the future include: leverage, liquidity, and pricing (marking to market). The leverage involved in derivatives is substantial; derivatives have wiped out capital and/or created maintenance calls that the holders (institutions) could not meet.

Later in this book we will discuss liquidity and the importance of making sure there are enough buyers and sellers in a market before a trade is placed. Unfortunately liquidity can dry up in a market, which forces buyers or sellers to accept losses to exit a trade. This is called the "roach motel" problem, where you can "check in" but you can't "check out."

The other problem Buffett pointed out is that many of these derivatives are on companies' books and their values are overstated. Additionally, the contra parties of some of the derivative instruments could be suspect in terms of fulfilling their contractual obligations. Part of the Enron mess was the company's use of derivatives and overstating the values of these instruments on its balance sheets.

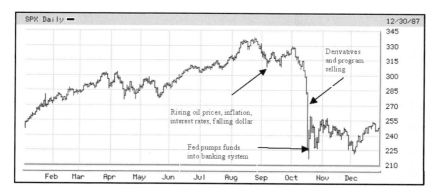

Figure 4.6: 1987 Stock Market Crash

The stock market crash of 1987 was one of those rare market meltdowns that was not followed by a recession. The Fed aggressively pumped money into the banking system which lowered rates and probably prevented a recession. The financial press and analysts blamed the crash on many factors including possible disruptions of oil due to the Iran-Iraq War, a falling dollar, and rising inflation and interest rates. These factors are the causes that led to the crash, but the selling became intense due to portfolio insurance, derivatives, and program selling.

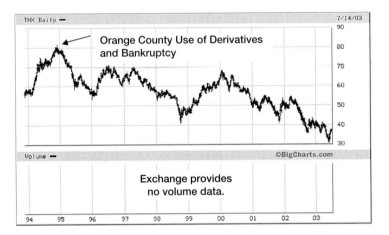

Figure 4.7: Yields for Ten-Year Treasury. Y-Axis Is Yield (Number /10)

As we can see in Figure 4.7, the yields for the ten-year treasuries went from around 5.75% to more than 8% in 1994. Yields and prices are inversely related. If you buy a bond paying 5% and rates go to 8%, you have to discount your bonds dramatically to attract investors to your lower-paying bond. This is what happened to investors in 1994. Rates were reversing all year, but the last straw was that Orange County, California's investments in derivatives created margin calls and forced Orange County into bankruptcy. If yields reverse, bond prices could get whacked again.

Table 4.1 shows the dramatic increase of prices for treasuries issued twenty years ago. The May 2014 13-1/4 bonds issued in 1984 are thirty-year bonds, and they are selling at a 56% premium. As rates fell the price increased from 100 to the price of the quote, 156:16. Notice how low the yields are. I anticipate seeing inflation and rising interest rates, and that the prices you see below would drop significantly lower as yields rise. Bond yields are examined further within in the inflation section later in this chapter.

Coupon	Maturity Month and Year	Bid	Ask	Change	Asked Yield
3 5/8	**May 13 n**	99:29	99:30	+10	3.63
12	**Aug 13**	145:07	145:08	+7	2.48
13 1/4	**May 14**	156:16	156:17	+6	2.71
12 1/2	**Aug 14**	153:24	153:25	+7	2.82
11 3/4	**Nov 14**	150:27	150:28	+9	2.90

Table 4.1: Ten-Year Treasury Quotes, Mid-2003   *n = note*

Figure 4.8: 1994 Impact of Orange County Bankruptcy on S&P 500

1994 was a difficult year for bond and stock investors. The year started with the Fed raising key interest rates. Later the Mexican peso was devalued, and toward the end of the year Orange County filed for bankruptcy protection, the largest municipal filing ever.

Figure 4.9 Russian Default and the Long-Term Capital Management Crisis

The Asian contagion and Russia's default on its government bonds created enormous problems for the money management firm known as Long-Term Capital Management (LTCM), for the Federal Reserve and major banks. The "elite" hedge fund had leveraged its equity of $4.8 billion into a $100 billion portfolio of derivatives. The fund was essentially short treasuries and long international debt securities. The Russian default caused investors to flee to treasuries and dump many international bonds. LTCM was stuck with huge losses, and its own selling to cover those losses made the problem even worse. In October the Federal Reserve Bank of New York arranged fifteen major banks to negotiate a bailout. Over the next few days central banks from around the world aggressively lowered rates and pumped up the money supply, and we were saved from a major financial crisis.

The Fed kept the United States out of recession for many years, but the tools of lowering interest rates and increasing the money supply is losing its effectiveness, and the capital markets keep creating bubbles.

U.S. Budget Deficits

Figure 4.10 is a shocking graph of our budget deficits which depicts how quickly we went from surpluses back to deficits. The war on terrorism, the new Homeland Security Department Programs, tax cuts, and the continued funding of expensive social programs are some of the reasons we are back in the hole. Many analysts expect the budget to get worse.

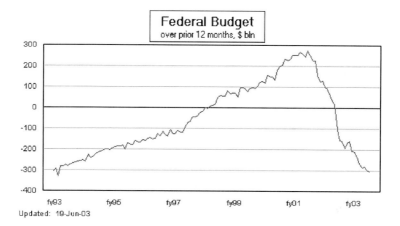

Figure 4.10: Federal Budget

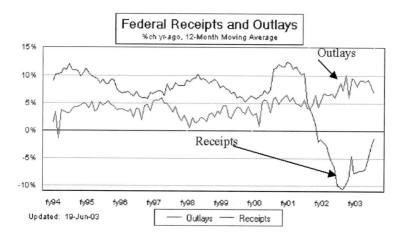

Figure 4.11: Federal Receipts and Outlays

We can see in Figure 4.11 that an increased growth rate in spending and lower tax receipts have put us right back into huge budget deficits. The budget deficits for 2003 at the time of this writing are estimated to grow to approximately $450 billion and even higher in 2004. Current Congressional Budget Office estimates project a deficit of $246 billion in 2003, and continued deficits through 2007.

Most economists agree that when our deficits go beyond 3% of our economy, the deficits become inflationary. This would be similar to having a $100,000 income and spending $103,000. This is fiscally irresponsible and financially unhealthy. The government will have to finance these debts, and they will have to use the capital markets and borrow money, crowding out other borrowers. To attract investors, the U.S. will have to raise rates. These deficits will add to our growing national debt. Now let's take a look at total debt in America.

The Debt Problem

The growing debt by consumers, corporations, and governments (federal, state, and local) is one of the worst economic problems the United States faces. In 1980 total aggregate borrowing totaled $4 trillion; by 2002 that debt had grown to $31 trillion dollars according to the Federal Reserve. This debt will certainly lead us to stagflation (a blend of stagnation and inflation); interest rates will be forced up to attract foreign dollars to finance our debts, and the higher rates and crushing debt will keep our economy in stagnation. This debt does not provide us much room for error, as any type of economic shock can be devastating to the U.S. economy.

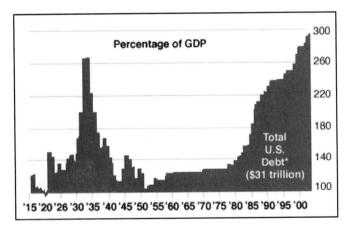

**Figure 4.12: Total Consumers', Corporate,
Government Debt as a Percent of GDP**

Figure 4.12 illustrates the growing debt problem. Debt as a percentage of GDP is greater than the ratio during the Great

Depression. The United States' financial condition is similar to a family living paycheck to paycheck that does not have an extra penny to spare or spend, and all income is used to pay bills, interest, and debt. If this family has an emergency, a major car or home repair, a serious illness in the family, then even one of these events could force the family into a much lower standard of living, force asset sales, or even bankruptcy. What happens to the family can happen to our economy on a much larger scale.

In the next chapter we discuss the growing indebtedness of consumers, and the drag that it causes the economy. The major theme of our book is that investors need gold in their portfolios, but our best advice is to pay down debt.

Source	$ Trillion
U.S. Govt.	$6.7
State & Local Govt.	$1.5
Mortgages	$5.8
Consumer Debt	$1.7
Corporate Debt	$5
Financial Institutions	$10
Total	**$30.7**

Table 4.2: Sources of Debt in the United States

Table 4.2 breaks down the sources of U.S. debt. What is very disturbing about this table is that a significant portion of the debt is from the government. We have close to an $11 trillion economy, and the government represents approximately 18% of it, but it owes 26% of the total debt.

The official U.S. government debt is approximately $6.7 trillion dollars. That is approximately $22,900 for each U.S. citizen. What's also scary is that a report commissioned by the U.S. Treasury Department shows the U.S. faces a future of chronic federal budget deficits totaling at least $44 trillion. The study is an assessment of how the U.S. government is at risk of being overwhelmed by the "baby boom" generation's future healthcare and retirement costs. The study's analysis of future deficits is significantly higher than previous estimates. Part of the problem is that current measures of the annual deficit and debt are misleading and archaic and do not reflect the total liabilities of future benefits that are expected. The study asserts that massive tax increases and budget cuts are needed. Everyone knows that this is politically impossible and it will probably never happen.

Rising Inflation

In the last few years the world economy has seen the trouble of a few high profile currencies like the Thai bhat and the Russian ruble.

To combat economic hardship central banks around the world have been lowering rates and increasing their money supplies into their economies. The impact of pumping huge amounts of money into an economy brings the problem of too many dollars chasing too few goods, i.e. inflation. Let's take a look at some disturbing trends we see in U.S. money growth and inflation.

In Figure 4.13 we can see the dramatic increase in the growth of the money supply since 1995. Many economists believe easy money is one of the main contributors to inflation.

M2 growth rate

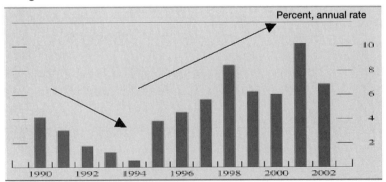

Note: M2 consists of currency, travelers checks, demand deposits, other checkable deposits, savings deposits (including money market deposit accounts), small denomination time deposits, and balances in retail money market funds.

Figure 4.13: Easy Money

In Figure 4.14 we can see the decline of the Consumer Price Index (CPI) and its recent reversal. The strongest price increases are in energy, food, housing, and commodity prices. Many economists are forecasting a slowing of home prices and sales but continued price increases for commodities and precious metals.

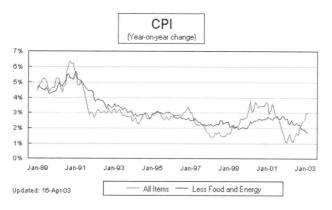

Figure 4.14: Trend of Inflation in the U.S.

You're probably asking yourself, if all this money is being pumped into the economy where is all that money going? Let's take a look:

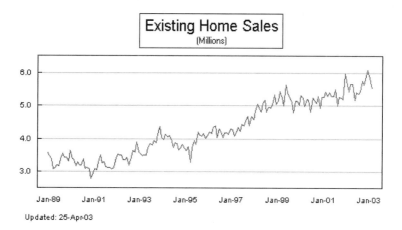

Figure 4.15: Existing Home Sales

Figure 4.16: Median Existing Home Prices

Figures 4.15 and 4.16 show us that a lot of money in the U.S. economy is going into home sales. We can also see the inflation in the prices of homes.

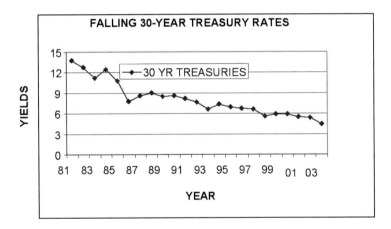

Figure 4.17: Trend of Falling Rates

We have inflation in bonds, higher prices and lower yields. A lot of the money supply has moved into bonds. Investors have rushed into bonds in the last few years because of their perceived safety, the weakening economy, and the prospects of lower rates. Historically there has been a 2%- to 3%-point spread between long-term government bonds and inflation. What bond yields are saying is that inflation will stay below 1.5%, an unlikely prospect. I believe that inflation will reverse, which can be very damaging to your bond holdings. If you need to sell your bonds you will have to lower the price of your bonds to compete with higher yielding bonds as inflation and interest rates rise. If interest rates move only one percentage point from 4% to 5%, you could lose up to 25% on your principal if you own very long-term, non-callable bonds. If you own bonds, make sure you protect yourself. The actions you should consider are taking profits, reducing your holdings, hedging with futures, or holding your bonds until maturity.

One of the concerns that stock market experts have is that with all this cheap money available, speculators have been borrowing short term to speculate in the markets. This can exacerbate market movements if rates do reverse. Borrowing short term to speculate is a profitable strategy as long as prices are rising, but once rates start to rise then borrowing costs start to go up, and asset prices start to fall. These speculators are forced to sell, creating even more selling in the bond and stock markets.

There is more than $5 trillion sitting in money markets. I really don't think investors know what a bad deal this is. The real return on money funds is negative. Money market yields are around 1% minus inflation; 1.5% minus taxes leaves you with a negative return. It would be wise to move some of your money from money market funds and bonds into gold. Gold is a safe haven and can protect you from imminent inflation.

The price of gold bottomed in the first quarter of 2001 and has been slowly climbing. There are a few causes offered to explain the increase, but many believe the change in the price of gold anticipates inflation. Alan Greenspan believes in the predictive value of inflation for gold. In the nineties he spoke before a congressional hearing and he cited gold as a "measure which has shown a fairly consistent lead on inflation." People want to hold real assets rather than financial assets when they think money's purchasing power will drop, Greenspan explained. As a gauge of inflation or inflationary expectations, gold is "better than commodity prices or a lot of other things," he added.

I have seen a few articles in the financial press and heard some Fed officials talking about deflation, and most admit this is a very remote possibility. I believe that even if we do see some deflation, gold could still do well because some of the money from the growing money supply will be invested in gold and investors will continue to seek gold in these uncertain and risky times.

Falling Dollar

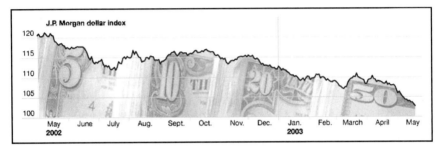

Figure 4.18: The Falling Value of the U.S. Dollar

Let me briefly explain to you the causes of the most recent falling value of the U.S. dollar. For many years, foreign investors and businesses moved money into the U.S. markets and economy based on the expectations of a healthy growing economy. A strong dollar is evidence of confidence in our economy and investment opportunities by our trading partners and investors.

This confidence has eroded, and the view of the United States as a place to conduct business and invest has changed for the following reasons:

- Stock market bubble burst

- September 11 terrorist attacks mean higher risk doing business in the U.S.

- Fed has lowered interest rates twelve times to historic lows, making dollar-denominated paper less worthwhile to hold

- Corporate scandals, negligent auditing firms and government regulators

- War on terrorism, including wars in Afghanistan and Iraq

- Twin deficits: the U.S. budget and trade balance (imports versus exports)

We have seen a net outflow of foreign investment money, causing downward pressure on the dollar and the U.S. stock markets.

I had mentioned that the lower value of the dollar is inflationary. Let's go over this again. For example, last year if I converted a U.S. dollar into a Euro I would have received one Euro. Now if the dollar is weaker and I convert one dollar into a Euro I need $1.20 to buy one Euro. A weaker dollar makes foreign goods more expensive, and reduces foreign competition, which leads to higher domestic prices. What normally can happen is domestic suppliers and manufacturers know foreign goods are more expensive, so they can raise their prices, potentially creating inflation. That's great news if you are a *producer* of goods in the U.S., but bad news if you are a *consumer* of goods. And inflation is even worse news if you are a bondholder.

If you're holding Euros or any other major foreign currency, dollar devaluation is good news. Let's say you have a Euro — you would be able to exchange one Euro for $1.20 U.S. dollars. The lower dollar value makes U.S. goods and services (including dollar denominated gold bullion) attractive to foreign investors. Foreign buyers are getting a 20% discount of U.S. goods and services, and that includes our rare gold coins.

Most other countries are wary of currency stability, as they have seen their own currency devalue, destroying their savings and purchasing power. This is especially true of large importing countries. These countries know the value of gold as a store of value. The U.S. economy imports represent only about 12% of our GDP, so devaluation is not as damaging. If the dollar continues to drop more than it already has, we will learn the impact of currency devaluation the hard way.

I think the weak dollar will be another impetus for inflation and that foreign investors will push up the prices of dollar-denominated gold investments. Also, if the value of the dollar gets too low, the Fed will be forced to raise rates to attract foreign money to finance our twin deficits, bad news for bond and stock investors.

Another important fact to remember is that historically, when citizens lose confidence in their country's currency, they seek gold as a safe haven.

Summary

I have spelled out the significant economic and terrorist threats the world faces. The Fed and world central banks are running out of ammunition to protect us. I have been motivated in the last few years to make changes to my portfolio, and I encourage you to also take steps to position yourself for the changing world and economy. You need to protect your wealth in case there is another terrorist attack here or with any of our allies and neighbors. Gold will protect your wealth and can hedge against inflation.

Later on we will examine the best ways to invest in gold and to hedge your gold portfolio. I will also explain what the best time is to buy gold, but more important, when you should sell.

Chapter 5
Why the Stock Market Will Continue to Provide Dismal Returns

I am very proud to be the publisher of one of this country's premier investment newsletters, *21st Century Investor.* I launched *21st Century Investor* in 1997, just as the biggest bull market in history was starting to gain steam.

Back then all you had to do was buy several high-quality technology stocks and hold them tightly and you made huge money. Many of the technology stocks that we recommended in *21st Century Investor* took off like rockets jumping 100%, 200%, and 1,000%. But the buy-and-hold strategy came to a screeching halt when the technology bubble in stocks finally burst.

In March of 2001 we were among the very first analysts to step forward and warn our subscribers that the United States was heading into a deep recession and that the buy-and-hold strategy had to be replaced with a "sell short strategy."

In the months that followed, our subscribers who took this advice racked up enormous profits shorting many of the top-tier technology stocks.

Clearly the success of *21st Century Investor* has been tied to our determination to not be solely bearish or bullish. We spend hundreds of hours researching economic indicators, examining charts and technical analysis, and researching the geo-political factors that provide the backdrop to the financial markets before we make our market calls.

Believe me when I say that no one wants a bull market more than I do; the investment newsletter business is much more profitable in a bull market than a bear market. It doesn't matter how much money you make subscribers in a bear market; there are always more subscribers and more profits in my business when the market is rising then when it is falling. A falling market breeds its own kind of mental depression and people reach the point where they don't even want to think about the market.

Unfortunately, our best research tells me that the bear market is not over. A new bull market is still on the horizon. This is not to say there are not great stocks that you can buy and make money investing in. In every bear market there are many wonderful investment opportunities that defy the bearish trend. For those opportunities, we encourage you to try a thirty-day free trial to 21stCenturyAlert.com, our one-stop investment research Web site dedicated to both long and short opportunities in the U.S. stock market.

We see the limited opportunities going forward for buy-and-hold investors. Most analysts have resigned themselves to this and many are suggesting diversification. There is too much risk in bonds unless you hold them to maturity, and money market funds give you a negative real return. We believe investors will continue to move into gold, pushing up prices.

We don't have to tell you how bad the markets have been for the 2000s. It is important to understand the causes of the bear market and why stock market professionals expect mediocre returns for the foreseeable future. Here are some of the factors causing the weakness:

- Reversing of falling inflation and interest rates
- Weak consumer confidence, high debt levels and a low savings rate
- Slower corporate profits
- Overcapacity
- Stagflation, similar to the stock market of the seventies
- Historically high valuations

The End of Falling Inflation and Interest Rates

In 1980 inflation was 13% and interest rates reached approximately 20%. If you had told investors that inflation would be close to 1% in 2001 and interest rates would be below 4% in 2003, you would have been called crazy. Inflation and interest rates have had an amazing decline since their peaks in the very early eighties.

Warren Buffett was interviewed in a major financial magazine in 1998 stating how the double-digit returns of the market would be over, that the returns would be mediocre and created with more risk. According to Buffett, the main contributors to the great bull market of the eighties and nineties were falling inflation and interest rates; with that economic trend behind us you will not see the gains we experienced in the eighties and nineties. Essentially when there is high inflation, investors will pay very little for earnings and stock prices because they know that the value will be eaten away by inflation. When inflation is low, investors will pay more for stocks because the earnings are likely to be from pure operations and do not have to be adjusted for inflation. Earnings can be considered wealth creators for corporations and investors.

The P/E (price/earnings) ratio is a reflection of what investors will pay for earnings. The P/E ratio is the stock price divided by its earnings per share. Let's say a stock is selling for $20 and has $1.25 in earnings. The stock would have a P/E of 16, which is $20/1.25. Again, the P/E is how much investors will pay for a company's earnings. In the example, the investor is willing to pay $16 for $1 of earnings. Stating it another way, if the P/E is 16 the "earnings yield" would be 1/16 or 6.25%.

Usually when inflation is low, less than 2%, investors are willing to pay up to $20 for a dollar of earnings. Historically inflation has averaged around 3%. A P/E would be about 17, so a stock with normal inflation would have a price of about $17 for $1 of earnings.

In periods of bad inflation a P/E can drop below 10, so a dollar's worth of earnings would be worth less than $10, almost half the price when inflation is low.

Let's look at valuations in 1980 and compare them with those of the 2000s.

Year	Inflation	Earnings	PE	Price
1974	12.3	99	6.2	616
1980	12.5	121.86	8	964
2000	3.4	485.14	22	10786
2002	2.4	386.62	21	8342
Forecast 2005	5	446	16	7136

Table 5.1: Dow, Then and Now

We can see in Table 5.1 that the market price level grew almost ten times from 1980 to 2000 thanks to rising earnings, falling inflation, and rising P/Es. We can also see that the P/E ratio as we write this is historically high; investment professionals have been warning about the high valuations of the market. We can also see that earnings declined from 484 in 2000 to 386 in 2002.

Historically the average growth rate of earnings for the Dow has been 7% per annum. This is expected to slow to 5% at best. These numbers do not include what would happen if we had another terrorist attack or a financial crisis. If inflation moves up to 5% as we anticipate and if earnings grow 5% over the next few years, the forecast for the Dow would be slightly above 7,000. In 2002 it did fall to 7200, so it would not be surprising to see the markets test this area again. The prospects for the market look very dim with the anticipated rising inflation and low earnings growth. Earnings growth is not strong enough to overcome rising inflation and contracting P/Es.

When I shared the Warren Buffett article with investors and investment professionals I know, all of them thought Buffett was way off, saying "things are different this time." His forecast in 1998 has turned out to be more than correct.

End of Falling Inflation and Interest Rates?

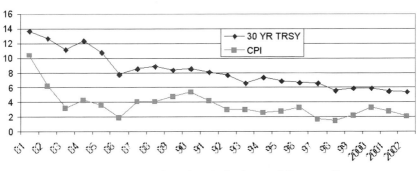

Figure 5.1: End of Falling Inflation and Interest Rates

Figure 5.1 shows the dramatic fall of interest rates and inflation over the last twenty years. As we discussed earlier, these trends are reversing and it is imperative to make adjustments to your portfolio. Rising inflation and interest rates are bad for stocks and bonds.

The Consumer Will Put a Damper on Economic Growth and Corporate Earnings

Consumers represent approximately 66% of the U.S. economy; therefore they have a major impact on the GDP, inflation, earnings growth, and the stock market. Low consumer confidence, a low savings rate, and high consumer debt levels will put a lid on economic activity and the stock market.

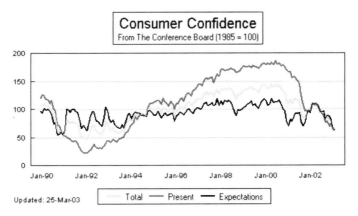

Figure 5.2: Consumer Confidence

Figure 5.2 exhibits the dramatic rise of consumer confidence in the nineties and the reversal in the 2000s.

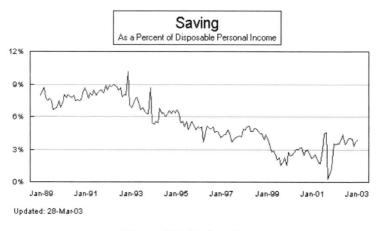

Figure 5.3: Savings Rate

Most healthy recoveries start with higher savings rates. Notice in Figure 5.3 how high the savings rate was during the last recession, and how low it is now. A low debt level, high savings rate, and lower interest rates at the beginning of an expansion can fuel economic growth and higher stock prices. We do not have those conditions in the current business cycle.

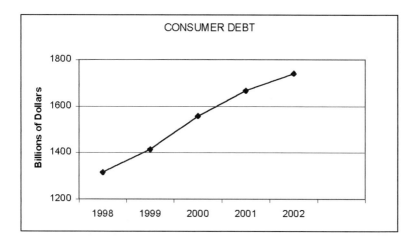

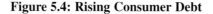

Figure 5.4: Rising Consumer Debt

Figure 5.4 shows the growing high debt levels of consumers. The high consumer debt levels and low savings rate leaves the economy without much growth potential and very vulnerable to economic shock.

Mediocre Earnings Growth

We have just learned that one of the main drivers of our economy and the stock market is the consumer, and we can't depend on the same growth from the consumer going forward.

In the late nineties, many corporations used aggressive accounting methods to meet high-growth earnings forecasts. It's a new day now for corporations because the Sarbanes-Oxley Act (corporate governance and auditing law), CEOs, CFOs, and shareholder demands are requiring accounting methods to be more conservative. This will add to the slow growth in earnings and limit the returns in the stock market. These are great developments for investors and are real positive changes for the long run.

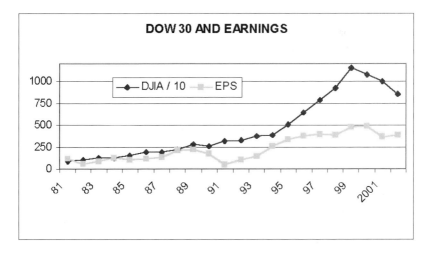

Figure 5.5: Dow 30 and Earnings

Figure 5.5 shows the important correlation between stock prices and earnings. We can see prices and earnings reverse; the earnings engine from the nineties stalled out in the 2000s. Notice that when price and earnings make a new move, stock prices lead the way. Prices were already heading down in 2000 before any troubles showed up in the earnings numbers.*

The capital markets in the late nineties directed trillions of dollars to Internet and technology companies and created asset bubbles. A lot of this money was used to build the Internet, Internet services, and fast digital networks for voice, data, music, and even movies. We have learned that too much capacity was built, which created an oversupply of digital networks, telecom equipment, and some technology hardware and software. Figure 5.6 illustrates the low growth of capital spending versus past recoveries.

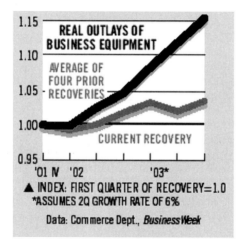

Figure 5.6: Capital Spending Weak in 2000s

This overcapacity has put pressure on margins, earnings, and revenues, and has allowed very little growth in technology. Many economists believe it will take years to work off the excess. Slow growth and weak earnings are not good for stock prices.

---

* *The point is that if you wait to see signs of trouble in the earnings numbers, the declining stock market will have already bitten you.*

Stagflation, 1970s Revisited

The conditions we just described are the ingredients for stagflation, a stagnant economy with inflation. We went through a similar period in the seventies; we can see below how it impacted the markets. The markets were stuck below 1,000 from 1966 to 1982. A trading strategy would have been more profitable than a buy-and-hold strategy.

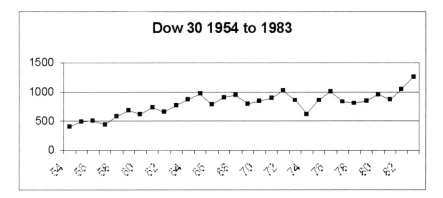

Figure 5.6: Dow 30, Stuck in a Range

The Dow was stuck below 1,000 from 1966 to 1982. Many experts believe that the market again will be stuck in a trading range.

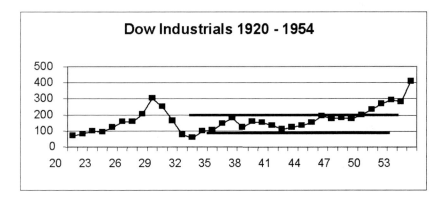

Figure 5.7: Dow 30, After Stock Market Bubble of 1929

The 1970s wasn't the only period during which the Dow was stuck in a trading range. It took over twenty years to reach the 1929 peak. The market was stuck below 200 from 1930 to 1949. A buy-and-hold strategy would not have worked during most of this period.

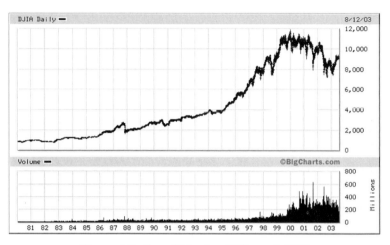

Figure 5.8: Dow 30 in the 1980s and 1990s

A buy-and-hold strategy would have made sense from 1980 to 2000 but not after 2000. Many Wall Street analysts believe we will experience similar trading markets as the seventies or as the period following the 1929 stock market crash. It's not too much of a stretch to imagine this. Figure 5.8 shows us that by 2003 the Dow is in its fifth year of being in the 7,000 to 11,000 range. The other major markets are also developing trading ranges.

The domestic stock market valuation peaked at $17.8 trillion in 2000 and it was approximately $11 trillion in 2003. In the early 2000s people invested in real estate, bonds, money markets and gold instead of owning shares in corporate America. Many investors lost trust in Wall Street because of the greed of corporate America's management and the failure of the accounting profession and government regulators to safeguard the individual investor. Many of these investors will not return to the stock market. Investors' willingness to take risks and invest in corporate America fueled economic growth and jobs in the nineties, and their unwillingness to come back to the stock markets could be another damper on the economy and the markets.

Many investors are realizing that a buy-and-hold strategy in the stock market no longer works, so they are diversifying out of stocks and into other investments that have greater potential such as gold.

High Stock Market Valuations

Analysts cite high P/E ratios and low dividend yields and other market valuation measures the factors that make this market historically expensive. Historically the stock market P/E is in the 14-16 range; the P/E for the S&P 500 for 2003 is 30. The usual dividend yield has been 3%, and in 2003 the S&P 500 dividend yield is 1.74%. There are normally two scenarios that can occur when stocks get expensive:

1. The market could fall further to historic averages where P/Es would be in the 16 range and dividends would be paying 3%. That means the market could continue lower.

2. The market could go sideways until earnings and dividends growth catch up with historical averages.

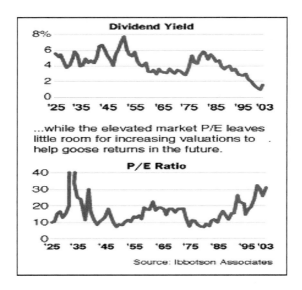

Figure 5.9: Historically High Valuations for Market

Figure 5.9 illustrates the historically high P/E and low dividend yield of the market even after a ferocious bear market.

Summary

Investors have been very disappointed with stock market returns in the 2000s. Unfortunately it is hard to believe that it will get any better or that we will ever see a return of the great bull market. Investors are starting to diversify, but many are not including gold yet. If you are still completely invested in stocks, I strongly urge you to reduce your stock holdings and start to diversify, and of course you should include gold in your portfolio

Eventually, I believe that a strong demand for gold will again come from the individual investor; and this strong demand will continue to increase the price of gold.

Chapter 6
The Changing Supply and Demand for Gold

The supply and demand picture for gold is absolutely compelling. I have not seen such a potentially explosive opportunity for gold since 1976. The last few chapters have focused on many causes of this new bull market in gold. Let's review some of those reasons:

- The war on terrorism and other global tensions will continue to cause uncertainty and stress among investors, and they will seek the safety of gold.

- Low interest rates and the rapidly expanding money supply in the United States and around the world are setting the stage for a massive inflationary wave. In an inflationary environment, even non-gold bulls will diversify into gold.

- Some of the money from huge increases in the money supply will continue to go into gold.

- Investment professionals are realizing the benefits of diversifying, mainly enhanced returns with lower risk. We discussed that gold is an excellent diversifier as it is unrelated to financial (paper) assets. Many portfolios, especially those controlled by big money managers do not have a gold component, and they will probably begin to allocate money into gold. A new equity gold trust fund will allow many investors including big money managers to participate in the gold market.

- The stock market pulled a lot of money away from other investments in the nineties, and the reverse is happening in the 2000s. As the stock market continues to perform poorly, more money from the stock market will likely be liquidated and some of those funds will be invested in gold.

The bull market in gold will be led by investor demand but there are other supply and demand forces that we have not discussed; they will also play a part in this bull market. Now let's examine these factors and determine why I believe gold will reach $1,000 an ounce.

Equity Gold Trust Fund Could Increase the Demand for Gold

As I write this, a subsidiary of the World Gold Council is working on a new exciting gold vehicle for investors. If you are familiar with Exchange Traded Funds (ETFs) then you will be more familiar with this subject matter. ETFs are similar to mutual funds in that they represent a share of a much larger portfolio. Currently many institutions and retirement accounts are barred from investing in gold because of the logistics for buying, storing, and insuring it. The Equity Gold Trust Fund would allow institutions and individual retirement accounts to legally and indirectly own gold. This could dramatically increase the demand for gold by opening up markets (currently closed). The amount of assets in institutions and retirement accounts is literally trillions of dollars.

Continued Strong Demand from Asia

Asian consumers and investors have always been big buyers of gold, especially during the last few years. They have a strong cultural, historical, and social preference for gold. In most Asian societies, individuals buy gold because it is a symbol of wealth and prestige. Dignity and pride are of extreme importance in Asian cultures, and gold fulfills those needs.

When European travelers and merchants visited the Far East over the centuries, they used gold as money to purchase goods. Asians tended to keep the gold; they did not use it to trade. They thought gold was too important to use as money. Their preference for real assets versus financial assets exists today because of their lack of trust in financial institutions and governments. Their country's borders, currencies, governments, and regimes have changed throughout history. These countries realize that gold can be a currency without borders and that it has held its value for thousands of years.

Gold experts say that Asians tend to buy gold when prices are low and do not sell their gold, so they tend to give gold some stability and support. These experts believe that Easterners own more gold than Westerners at this point in history. Many Americans and Europeans still view gold as an investment and are very concerned about its appreciation potential. Americans buy gold when the appreciation potential is good, during times of global tension and anticipated inflation.

Table 6.1 lists the countries/continents that are the biggest buyers of gold.

Country	2002 Demand in Tons
India	575.7
USA	409.3
SE Asia	256.5
Europe	239.3
China	202.3
Gulf States	145.7
Saudi Arabia	143
Japan	141.5
Turkey	128.4
Egypt	117.4

Table 6.1: Gold Demand in Key Countries

Let's examine the important trends developing in India and China more closely.

India

We can see in Table 6.1 that India is the largest buyer of gold in the world. India uses gold as a form of portable wealth. Indians spend more on gold than on cars and other consumer items. Gold is the only form of savings and investments for many Indians. Indian women are big collectors of gold and gold jewelry; it is a way for them to save and accumulate wealth.

China

Many gold experts anticipate strong demand from China due to deregulation and China's growing importance as an emerging economy. The gold market in China was tightly controlled by the Chinese government until recently. In October of 2002 the Shanghai Gold Exchange opened, and in 2003 the rules governing both domestic and international participation in the gold fabrication market in China were relaxed.

Chinese GDP growth in the early 2000s has been the fastest growing in the world. It has been consistently expanding above the 7% range. In 2001 China had the seventh-largest economy at $1.16 trillion. They also have the largest population with more than 1.27 billion citizens, almost one billion more than the U.S. According to a study on the World Gold Council Web site, private financial assets stand at about $1.208 trillion. China has been admitted to the important World Trade Organization (WTO), which will continue to help China become an important economy in the world. The World Gold Council study also states that China's industrial and investment demand for gold is projected to increase dramatically in the future, now that gold is in the process of being deregulated.

To summarize, demand for gold by China will dramatically increase due to:

1. Historical and cultural preference for gold

2. Deregulation

3. Large population

4. Growing and important economy, and its admission to the WTO

The demand for gold by India, China, and Asia is expected to stay strong.

Total Demand for Gold Continues to Increase

I predict that the biggest demand for gold will continue to come from investors looking to protect their wealth from potential terrorist attacks or a financial crisis, or as an inflation hedge. It's also important to discuss the other sources of demand for gold, as I believe that demand from those areas will continue to grow as well.

Source of Gold Demand	Tons
Jewelry	2,726.7
Retail investment	340.7
Industrial	278.4
Dental	68.7
Total	3,414.5

Table 6.2: Total Gold Demand, 2002

Table 6.2 shows us that demand for gold was approximately 3,414 tons in 2002. In 1990 the total demand for gold was 2,239 tons, so in 12 years we have seen an almost 50% increase in total demand for gold, and this was during a period of falling prices.

Most of the demand for gold is met by new production, which was approximately 2,600 tons in 2002. The rest of the supply to meet demand comes from central bank sales and gold scrap. Most gold analysts believe that the *demand* for gold will continue to rise for the reasons stated, but the new *supply* of gold will decline.

Figure 6.1 shows us that gold production has leveled off during the last few years and has even declined. Let's now see why supply is declining and what the prospects are for the supply of gold.

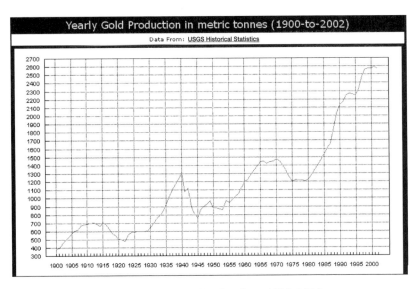

Figure 6.1: Gold Production, 1900-2002

Notice in the graph above how production took off for gold once the price of gold was allowed to float in 1975. Also notice that production has leveled off since 1997.

The Supply of Gold

Another big reason I believe gold prices will increase is because demand will outstrip supply. We saw in the last section that the production level of gold has plateaued and is starting to decline. I believe this trend will continue for the following reasons:

- Bear market in gold is over so the selling will end

- Central bank selling is known and will be less than in the nineties

- Forward contract selling by producers will continue to subside

- Consolidation in the gold mining industry will reduce the amount of exploration and production of gold

- Gold exploration is expensive and takes time to bring to production, so production is slow to respond to price movements

- South African mines, the world's largest producers, will continue to have reduced production

From 1996 to 2001, gold had increasing supply (new supply contracting) and thus a bear market for gold ensued. There were several causes of the gold trends in the 1990s, and I see those forces reversing:

1. Investment dollars attracted to U.S. bull market and high real returns from U.S. treasuries

2. Selling by central banks

3. Short selling by speculators

4. Forward contract selling by producers and other hedgers

I mentioned before that I started publishing in the stock market newsletter business at the right time. I saw money flowing into the market and investors making a lot of money, and I saw two industries flourish: Internet and biotechnology. The good thing about the bull market was that it financed the potential of the Internet, and the Internet has changed the way we invest, learn, and how we entertain ourselves. Money also poured into biotechnology which helped fund the sequencing of the human genome, and every day scientists learn more about life, disease, and cancer.

In the late 1990s I witnessed investors pulling money out of their conservative mutual stock funds, bonds, and real estate and putting that money into growth stocks like the Internet and biotechnology stocks. Gold, bonds, and real estate were the last place investors wanted to put their money. Now in the early 2000s we have seen investors pull money out of the market and move the money into bonds and real estate, and I believe some of that money will find its way into gold.

Central banks also started realizing that the real returns (interest rates minus inflation) in certain government bonds were positive and they started liquidating their gold reserves in favor of buying government-backed interest-bearing securities. Ironically, they did this just in time to see interest rates fall to a multi-decade low. Central banks are an important source of supply and demand. Let's take a closer look at central banks and gold reserves.

Central Banks

More than 100 years ago, the major economies around the world were on the gold standard and the majority of the central banks' reserves were in gold. Today with increased trade and the evolution of financial markets most central bank reserves are in foreign currencies in the form of short-term government securities.

Most central banks hold gold as part of their reserve assets. Of the 176 central banks reporting to the International Monetary Fund at the end of 2001, 102 (58%) declared some gold holdings, and only 11 (6%) declared they did not hold gold. The remaining 63 countries did not declare either way.

Table 6.3 lists the countries and financial entities with the largest gold reserves.

Country or Financial Entity	Tons
United States	8,149
Germany	3,446
International Monetary Fund	3,217
France	3,025
Italy	2,452

Country or Financial Entity	Tons
Switzerland	1,888
Netherlands	843
European Central Bank	767
Japan	765
Mainland China	600

Table 6.3: Top Ten Gold-Holding Countries and Financial Entities

Central banks had convinced themselves in the nineties that the dollar was a stable and good place to store their reserves. Certain central banks were heavy sellers of gold in the late 1990s, causing a deep slide in gold prices. There is an agreement through September 2004 by the central banks to limit sales to 400 tons per year. This removes the uncertainty faced by the gold market in the late 1990s. I believe that much of this selling is over, as the major motive to buy U.S. dollars because of its strength has reversed.

Central bank sales depressed the price of gold and caused even more selling by investors, short selling by speculators, and the selling of forward contracts by producers. These activities have abated.

Forward Contract Selling by Producers

We will discuss hedging techniques for gold in a later chapter. Here we will briefly explain selling of gold in the futures market. Over the years, the futures market has developed hedging vehicles for many commodities, financial assets, energies, base metals, and precious metals like gold. There were a lot of forward contract sales during the recent bear gold market, and these sales were meant to hedge long gold positions or future production. A futures contract is a contract sold on an exchange and has fixed specifications. A forward contract is a non-exchange contract and is customized for the two parties involved.

Let's say you own a gold mining company, and you see central banks unloading gold to capture higher interest rates in the government bond market. The selling will mean lower prices for gold. Briefly, here are the steps the gold mining company could take to hedge its position:

1. Sell gold for delivery in six months at today's current price of $400. The gold mining company locks in a price of $400 with a seller for delivery in six months.

Then, six months later, the price of gold falls to $300.

2. Because the company sold at $400 with a forward contract, all the company has to do is deliver the gold to the buyer of the contract when the contract expires. The company avoids the loss because it hedged and sold its gold with a forward contract for $400. The company delivers the gold and it will receive $400 per ounce. The amount of ounces is specified in the contract.

Again we will explain how hedging and the futures market works.

In the mid- to late-1990s there was certainly an incentive to sell futures to hedge gold holdings. As suppliers rushed to hedge by selling futures contracts or forward contracts, prices sank even lower. As the price of gold has increased, forward futures selling has diminished.

South African Production Will Continue to Decline

35% of the world's identified gold resources are in South Africa; however, gold production is likely to continue to decrease as it has been doing since its peak production days of the 1970s. Even though production is declining, the amount is still significant; South Africa will continue be a major producer of gold.

Figure 6.2 illustrates that as gold entered a bear market in 1996, the decline in gold production accelerated.

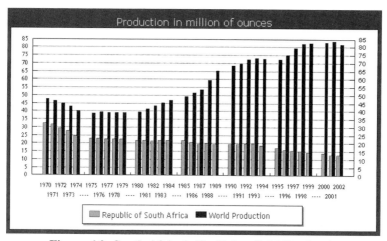

Figure 6.2: South Africa's Declining Gold Production

South Africa's mines are much larger and much deeper than most gold mines in the world. Today much of the mining is at very deep levels, as much as 13,000 feet or more below sea level. The cost to mine at these levels is very expensive, partly due to air conditioning costs, and the ore is of lower grade. The easier-to-access and less expensive gold in South Africa has already been mined.

When the cost of gold fell below $350, there was very little incentive for South Africa to produce gold.

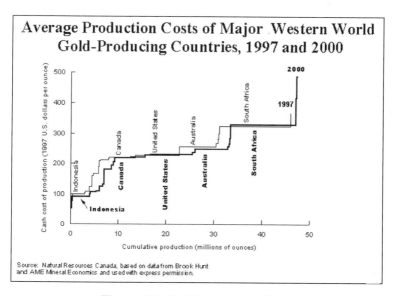

Figure 6.3: Gold Production Costs

Figure 6.3 shows the lowest cost producers to the highest cost producers, and just as important, the largest and smallest producers. We can see that South Africa is the largest producer with the highest costs. This chart is important because we can see that for most producers the cost of gold production is around the $250-per-ounce area. This price has been a very important support level.

Consolidation of Gold Industry Will Decrease Supply

Typical mining costs are $238 per ounce on average, but these costs can vary widely among producers depending on mining type and ore quality. When prices fall below these levels there is no incentive to produce gold. As we can see in Figure 6.4, gold did fall to these levels and many producers did stop producing and exploring for gold. When the price of any commodity drops below cost, what tends to happen is that producers will stop production, a shortage will occur, and eventually prices will shoot up as demand picks up or world tension or inflation is anticipated. Most commodities and precious metals go through stages of surplus with falling prices to shortages with increasing prices.

Spot gold, Jan 2 1992 to date

Figure 6.4: Gold Bear Market

In Figure 6.4 we can see that the *price* of gold held at the $250 level, close to the average *cost* to produce gold.

Many gold mining companies struggled during the gold bear market. As we saw earlier, gold production is actually declining; this also reflects the aging of existing mines and the likelihood that few mines will start up due to a consolidation in the gold mining industry. Some of the big gold mining companies like Battle Mountain Creek, Homestake, and Echo Bay Mines no longer exist because they have been bought out by rivals.

It's not only difficult to find new gold, it's also expensive. A survey by Toronto-based Beacon Group found that worldwide gold production by 2010 could be nearly 30% less than in 2001. Even if prices rise, supply will still be an issue because of the difficulty and time required to find gold. In an interview in a major investment publication, Joseph Foster, manager of the Van Eck International Investors Gold Fund and a former geologist, confirms how difficult and expensive it is to find gold: "Mines are hard to find; I can tell you from experience. I've drilled a lot of dusters."

Summary of Increasing Demand and Declining Supply for Gold

Let's summarize all the reasons why increased demand and reduced supply will continue to increase the price of gold.

Demand

Investor needs:

- Diversification: low returns from stock market, money markets, bonds

- Safe haven from world tension, financial crisis

- Inflation hedge

- Gold Equity Trust Funds and other vehicles will expand the number of potential investors for gold

- Continued strong demand from Asia, especially India and China

Fabrication needs:

- Continued strong demand for jewelry and industrial uses

Decreased supply

- Decreased production from gold bear market

- Consolidation in industry will create less exploration and production of gold

- The exploration of gold is time and capital intensive

- South Africa, the world's largest gold producer, will continue to produce less

- Gold sales from central bankers, hedgers, investors, speculators are diminishing

Gold at $1,000

While it's true I'm a gold bull and I believe gold will rise to $1,000 an ounce in the next few years, it's important to point out that we may see this price level attained as the result of a slow steady rise in the price of the yellow metal or as the result of one or more acute catalysts. The remaining section of this chapter is a detailed scenario on how gold could potentially reach $1,000.

Growing money supply will lead to inflation, the lower dollar, and/or another oil shock: Former Federal Governor Wayne Angell was quoted in *The Wall Street Journal* saying that historically for every anticipated .2% of inflation gold increases by $10. Given the tremendous growth rate in the money supply, thanks to the relaxed monetary policy of the Federal Reserve, it's very likely that over the next eighteen to thirty-six months we'll see a 5% increase in the rate of inflation. That would be about a 3% increase from levels of the early 2000s; assuming gold is at $365 in 2003 that would raise the price of gold to $515 (3/.2 * $10 + $365).

Let's examine the two possible and very likely catalysts that would cause a dramatic rise in the price of gold.

Catalyst #1: A second major terrorist attack on the United States' mainland. The September 11, 2001 terrorist attacks on New York and Washington were devastating. A second terrorist attack in the United States would send the dollar into a precipitous fall and the price of gold could easily leap to more than $600 an ounce.

In the event of a nuclear, chemical, or biological attack here in the United States or in Europe against one of our allies, the price of gold could soar to more than $1,000 in a matter of hours.

Catalyst #2: A major financial catastrophe. I discussed the major financial crises we have faced over the years. Wall Street has always faced scandals but never on the scale that we saw in the 2000s, and there are probably more to come. I also mentioned derivatives, which were responsible for market disruptions in the stock market crash of 1987, the Orange County, CA bankruptcy in 1994 and the Long-Term Capital Management debacle in 1998. Don't miss the obvious here. If investors are hit with another major financial crisis, it will act as a tremendous catalyst for gold.

The 1987 stock market crash caused a strong rise in gold. When the market peaked in August, gold was at $456 per ounce and it rose to $491 per ounce by December 1987, when the stock market made its final bottom.

The power of these two sudden catalysts cannot be understated because they would both cause a tremendous buying frenzy fueled by short covering and speculative momentum buying.

There's a principal of investing I have learned that has proven itself over and over again: "Markets move much further, up or down, than anyone can anticipate."

A few examples of this:

The 1980 gold market: No one would have believed in 1976 that gold would hit $850 just four years later…

The 1995-2000 bull stock market: In 1995 I remember my previous publisher, a perennial bear, laughing at me when I told him I thought the Dow would top 10,000. He and many others considered that impossible.

The 2000-2003 collapse of the Nasdaq: 5,000 to less than 1,100. Need I say more?

When the "frenzy stage" hits the gold market in the next few years, greed will run rampant. Gold will be mentioned not only in the financial press every day but in the mainstream media. Speculators and momentum traders will jump on board like locusts, and the price of gold will jump every day!

Short sellers who did not believe in the run-up will be forced to buy back and add to a buying panic. Once gold breaks through its old high of $850, there is no longer any supply or resistance; gold could easily reach $1,000 during this last phase. I have seen this process happen to many markets and to stocks, and I could easily see this happening to gold. By the way, this scenario is similar to the conditions of the 1970s and in 1980, except now there are trillions of dollars more in investable funds globally (in the U.S. alone in 1980 the total market value of all U.S. securities was approximately $1.5 trillion and today it is approximately $11 trillion) and millions more potential investors than the last gold bull cycle. Table 6.4 shows the big differences between the number of investors, gold vehicles and money available to fuel a major bull market in gold.

	1980	**2003**
U.S. Equity Market Value	$1.5 trillion	$11 trillion
U.S. Population	226,546,000	281,421,906
Investors	16 million	48 million
Gold Mutual Funds	Less than 10	18+
Indices	0	6
	Communism	Global Capitalism
China Population	981,200,000	1,273,111,290
China Private Financial Assets	?	$1.208 trillion

Table 6.4: Changes Which Fuel a Bull Market in Gold, 1980-2003

If we see just 5% move from stocks to gold in the U.S. and 5% from China's private assets, this alone would cause prices to double. The new equity gold trust fund could be the vehicle that investors use to invest in gold.

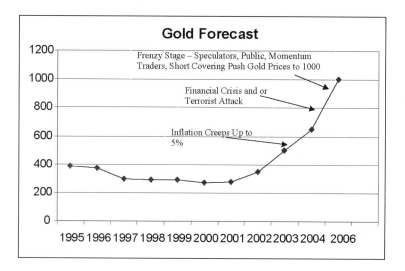

Figure 6.5: Gold Forecast. (The possible scenario where gold would reach $1,000)

Investors and speculators who buy gold below $500 will enjoy at least a two-to-one return on their money. We'll explore both conservative and aggressive ways to invest and speculate in gold including a few ways to leverage the coming bull market in gold.

Chapter 7
When to Buy and Sell Gold

Introduction

The first section of this book builds the compelling case for gold as an investment and lists the many reasons why gold could easily reach $1,000 per ounce in the next few years. In this section I will focus on the nuts and bolts of gold investing. The gold investment opportunities have increased dramatically since the last gold bull market. I will discuss and explain the many investment vehicles from which investors have to choose, covering the conservative to the aggressive, gold coins to financial futures, so that you can determine which gold vehicle is right for you. I will also answer the very important questions below; they are questions you should ask and answer with every investment, including your gold investment:

1. What to buy?

2. Why?

3. When to buy?

4. How to hedge?

5. When to sell?

My personal library includes many investment and gold books. Most books focus on *what* to buy and *why*, but very few discuss *when* to buy and even fewer tell you when to *sell* or how to *hedge*. This chapter will help you with the very important decisions of when to buy and when to sell. We'll cover the remaining questions in later chapters.

When to Buy

As mentioned in the previous section, any price below $500 would give you a risk/reward relationship better than 2/1, so you should begin your initial investment in gold immediately if you can buy gold below $500.

There is an investment "rule" that always seems to be at work — one that all investors can relate to: "If I buy something today, the price will be lower tomorrow; and if I sell something today the price will be higher tomorrow." For most of us this is a reality. It helps to *build* a position in an investment rather than buying it all at once. Let's assume you made your initial investment in gold below $500. Now how do we maximize your next purchase? We will use a discipline called technical analysis. Technical analysis (TA) is the study of the movements of prices through time. Technical analysts employ price charts and a variety of indicators to help forecast the future direction of price movements. TA is very helpful in answering the question of when to buy and sell. In this section, we will teach a few basic concepts of TA to help you with your buying and selling whether you are buying coins, bullion, indexes, mutual funds, futures or options.

Technical analysis is one of the oldest tools available to investors; its roots date back to the 1600s, when the Japanese used candlestick charts to analyze and forecast the price of rice. One of the helpful aspects of TA is that it can identify the extremes of fear and greed in the markets, which are certainly factors in gold's price movement as with any asset. When you see the extremes of fear and greed in long-term price charts, they normally indicate a long-term trend nearing an end.

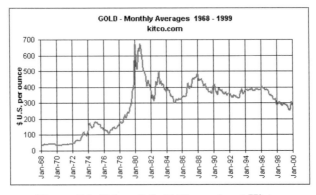

Figure 7.1: Price of Gold Throughout History

We can see in Figure 7.1 the long-term price fluctuations of gold. Notice the fear and greed in the chart. The almost vertical ascent of gold from 1978 to 1980 is obviously greed in the gold market. We think this could occur again. We can also see panic in the market as prices collapsed to the $300 level in 1982.

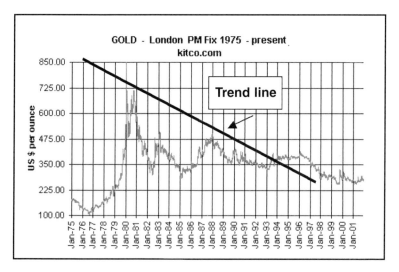

Figure 7.2: Downward Trend in Price of Gold, 1975-2002

Figure 7.2 indicates the downward trend in the price of gold. For gold to break out of the bear market, it would have to break through the long-term trend line.

There are many important tenets of technical analysis. I will explain a few that can be of help with your buy and sell decisions: the importance of time, trend identification, and trend lines.

Trends are essentially the direction of the collective rallies and pullbacks of prices.

Prices are either going up, down, or moving sideways. As a trader you want to position yourself to profit in the direction of the trend. As traders and investors say, "The trend is your friend." We can see that from 1977 to 1980 the long-term trend was up; every rally took prices higher and when selling occurred, price lows were higher than the previous lows. We had higher highs and higher lows;

traders and investors were buying the pullbacks and taking prices higher. After 1980, we had the *reverse* of this. Every rally was met with selling, so rallies were lower and each pullback went lower than the previous low; we had lower highs and lower lows. There were several periods were gold was stuck in a very narrow range, such as the period from 1998 to 2002.

Time is a very important concept in TA. A short-term trend is considered three weeks or less, a medium-term trend is considered three weeks to three months, and a long-term trend is considered longer than three months to years or even decades. Long-term trends dominate the medium- and short-term trends. The long-term trend in Figure 7.2 is down.

Here is how you draw a trend line: If prices are heading down, causing lower highs and lower lows, then a trend line is drawn tying the tops of the rallies together in a straight line. In Figure 7.2 the downward sloping trend line is considered resistance for rally attempts. If prices are moving up making higher highs and higher lows then to determine the trend line you would tie the bottoms together in a straight line like we did in Figure 7.3. If prices break through the trend line by 3% to 5%, then the existing trend is considered to have reversed.

Figure 7.3: Gold Breaking Out of Long-Term Down Trend

Once gold breaks out of the long-term trend line, gold is considered entering into a new bull market. Let's get back to when to buy. In Figure 7.3 we can see the new bull market started to begin after the bottom in April 2001. But it did not break out of the bottoming range until price moved above the long-term trend line. The new upward trend line now represents support. The time to buy is when prices pull back to the trend line. Let's take a closer look at the upward trend of gold.

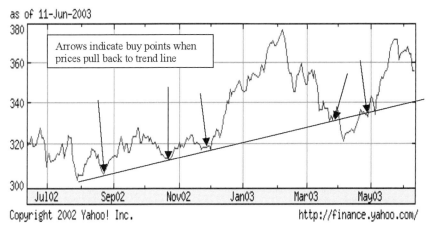

Figure 7.4: Buy Points for Gold Using a Trend Line

The chart above with its trend line indicates the buy points, when prices pullback to the trend line. During this one-year period there were quite a few opportunities to buy gold at good prices. We can try and anticipate the next time prices would pull back to the trend line and it looks like that would be in the $340 to $350 area. You can try to place your next buy order at those prices. You can adjust your buy order as prices get closer to the trend line.

Some technicians do not like using trend lines, so they use moving averages which are very popular among traders and investors. A moving average (MA) is the smoothing of a trend. By definition it is an average of prices over a time frame, and it moves as the trend moves. Its purpose is to identify and track the progress of a trend.

We already mentioned that time is important in technical analysis. There are also different moving averages for different time frames. For the short-term, technicians may use a 10-day moving average. Since each week has five trading days, a 10-day moving average is two weeks, and that is the time frame for short-term trends. The 50-day MA is very common and is equivalent to six weeks for medium-term time frames; a 200-day moving average is normally used for long-term trends. A moving average's length should be set at about one half of the period of the oscillation you are trying to take advantage of.

For your second purchase you normally buy when the prices move above the MA. We will explain and illustrate later how to use moving averages and trend lines for sell signals. Because you would probably want to make your second purchase as soon as possible, you should probably use a 10-day moving average. Some technicians use a 10-day MA as a proxy for a trend line.

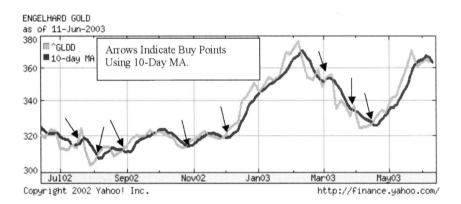

Figure 7.5: Using 10-Day Moving Average to Enter a Buy Order for Gold

The chart above is a one-year chart using a 10-day moving average. Technicians would enter into a position when prices (the dotted line), cross above the MA line (the solid line). The 10-day MA follows prices fairly closely; it would have given us at least eight buy signals to buy gold.

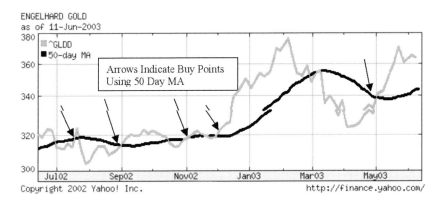

Figure 7.6: Using a 50-Day Moving Average to Enter a Gold Position

The 50-day moving average in Figure 7.6 gave us five buy signals. The MA is medium-term and does not follow prices as closely, so the signals are fewer. Prices have to pull back a little bit more to trigger a buy signal. Sideways periods like 2002 will generate a lot of signals that don't seem to go anywhere, but following them can ensure you don't miss the beginning of a general up move like we saw in late 2002 and early 2003.

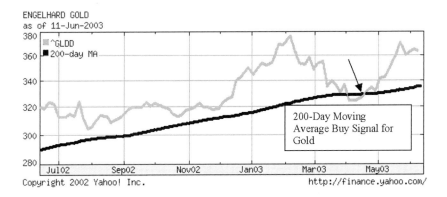

Figure 7.7: 200-Day Moving Average, Buy Signal for Gold

A 200-day moving average is used to determine long-term trends and to help identify long-term buy and sell points. As we can see in Figure 7.7, we do not get many signals using the 200-day moving average. The signals do not occur often, but they are normally very good signals to enter and could be used to add positions.

Using moving averages can help you with your buy decisions. The 10-day MA will make sure you get in, and the 50- and 200-day MA can help you add to your positions.

Technicians certainly use other indicators and tools to help them with their buy and sell decisions, but those indicators are beyond the scope of this book. The trend line and MA are easy enough to use and learn and are very popular. Because so many investors and traders use trend lines and MAs, the signals almost become self-fulfilling. This is one of the reasons why these indicators are useful. Of course, prices can go below the buy points, as we have seen, but the idea is to get in at a good price when we believe prices will eventually move significantly higher.

It is very normal for prices to make a move and then go sideways. There are many names for these sideways movements, such as *trading range, consolidation, congestion, rectangles, non-trending, trendless,* etc. These periods of sideways movement are normally rest periods in the long-term movement and they can occur at round-numbered areas, for example: $250, $300, $350, $400, etc. Don't be surprised to see consolidations during gold's climb to $1,000. Figure 7.8 shows several examples of periods of consolidation.

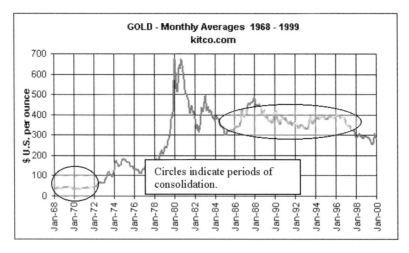

Figure 7.8: Periods of Gold Prices in Trading Range

Selling Gold

You probably would not want to sell all your gold. Gold has historically done well when financial assets don't, so you should always have some gold for a balanced, efficient portfolio.

One good strategy is to sell half your position once you have doubled your money. Gamblers in Las Vegas call this "playing with the house's money." For example, let's say you were astute in your buying and your average cost was $350. When it reaches $700 sell half your position. There are advantages to this strategy. Now with less risk and more conviction, you can stay for the last stage of the trend, the frenzy stage, or what technicians call the distribution phase. This is also the riskiest and most volatile phase of the trend. By taking your original capital off the table while still having a position, you are better off psychologically to take advantage of the last and potentially most profitable stage of a trend.

We are going to closely examine the last bull market in gold to learn how we would exit profitably. The new bull market should look very similar except the high will probably be $1,000 instead of $850.

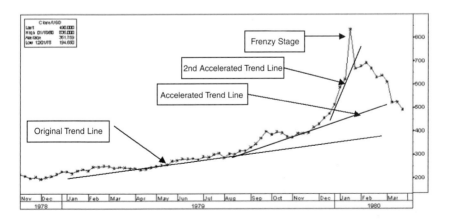

Figure 7.9: Long-Term Chart of Gold Run-Up in Late 1970s, 1980

Figure 7.9 shows the bull market more than twenty years ago. The chart has several trend lines drawn; technicians redraw trend lines as they accelerate or decelerate. The technique is called fanning.

1. The original trend line has a sustainable ascent. Again we tie the lows together with a straight line.

2. We need to draw a second trend line as prices accelerate from the original trend line. Trend lines act as support for a trend; we can see that as prices pull back in March of 1980, prices find support at the trend line in the $500 area.

3. The third trend line ascent will be very hard to maintain. The higher the ascent, the easier it is for prices to break the trend line; and once prices significantly break the trend line, the trend will normally reverse.

4. The frenzy stage is the last stage of a trend, as the ascent is just not sustainable; and the ascent seems to approach 90-degree angles. Round numbers become important resistance points to look at. In this chart the $850 area will be an important resistance point that the current bull market will have to take out. The frenzy area is the area that we wait to exit, even though the waiting is difficult. And selling just when everything seems to be going great is even more difficult.

Now let's take a closer look at the reversal of this trend, as it will give us some insight on how we may exit in the new gold bull market.

One important rule I have learned regarding investing is to forget trying to pick a bottom or a top in prices; it is a futile effort that leads many people to miss profit opportunities.

Our sell strategy will be similar to our buy strategy. We know that we will not be able exit at the exact top, so we will use a short-term moving average to make our first exit and a medium- or long-term MA to help us exit the rest of our positions.

Figure 7.10: Accelerated Trend Lines for Gold in 1980

When prices accelerate as they normally do in the frenzy stage, the trend will be easy to break and you should be ready to take profits. In the frenzy stage prices will have doubled. Once prices move in a strong 90-degree angle you should use a very short-term moving average to help you make your first initial liquidation; here we will use a five-day MA. We want to sell when prices move below the five-day MA. As you can see we would have not sold at the highest price, and most people don't, but we would probably get out at a very good price around the $700 area.

Some traders will also use a 50-day or 200-day moving average to help them out of the rest of their positions. This is a good idea. Figure 7.10 shows that the five-day MA was the first signal, but the other MAs did not trigger a sell signal. Because the short-term MA will give you an early signal to exit, sometimes prices can recover and go higher; so professional traders like using longer-term MAs for the rest of their positions. If prices go below the longer-term MA, then it is a good sign that the long-term trend is over and they will exit their remaining positions.

Notice that by the end of February most MAs are moving down indicating that the up trend is getting close to being over. Prices finally move below the 50-day moving average and then prices really break down to the $500 level.

Summary

Here is a quick summary for the important "when to buy and sell" decisions.

When to buy:

1. Start your initial purchase immediately if prices are below $500.

2. Use a trend line or a 10-day moving average to make your next purchase. Buy with the trend line when prices *pull back* to the trend line. Buy with the moving average when prices move *above* the MA line.

3. You can also use the 50-day and 200-day moving average to make subsequent buys.

The short-term signals will ensure you are positioned; the longer-term signals will help you add support to your positions.

When to sell:

1. Wait for the frenzy stage: Gold prices have more than doubled, gold is on the nightly news, and the front page of the newspaper and price charts show prices in a 90-degree ascent.

2. Use a five-day MA in the frenzy stage to give you a sell signal. Sell when prices move below the five-day MA line.

3. It is a good idea not to sell all of your gold with the first liquidation, as prices could recover and go higher. Use a 50-day MA to liquidate the remaining gold you do not want to own. It is a good idea to keep some gold to balance your stock portfolio.

These buy and sell skills can be helpful in your buying and selling decisions for gold, gold stocks, and mutual funds, especially futures and options. Technical analysis is used to buy and sell any asset that has price charts.

We are now ready to examine specific gold investment vehicles.

Gold and the Presidential Cycle

I would like to share with you a relatively unknown fact about gold and presidential cycles. The best time to buy gold is normally one year before a presidential election, like 2003, 2007, 2011, etc. One explanation for the seasonality may be that an incumbent president and his administration will do everything they can to boost the economy, so by election year the economy is normally doing much better and inflation is heating up.

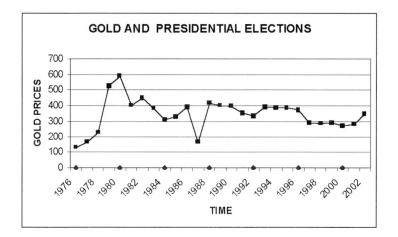

Figure 7.11: Gold and Presidential Elections

Starting with 1975 when individuals were able to own gold in the U.S., if you would have bought gold the year before an election, gold appreciated every election year except in 1996.

Figure 7.11 indicates that buying gold in 2007 could be a good timing decision.

Chapter 8
Forty-Year Gold Rush Cycles

Contributions by: Tom McClellan

I was fortunate enough to have Tom McClellan help me with this book. This chapter was primarily written by Tom. His research in gold has led him to identify a forty-year gold rush cycle in gold prices. Tom and his father, Sherman, are very well known in the investment community for their famous "McClellan Summation Index" and "McClellan Oscillator." I proudly offer their excellent newsletter to our subscribers. You can subscribe and follow their important research and investment advice online at www.21stcenturyalert.com.

In previous chapters, you have read about the various reasons why we should expect a new bull market in gold prices. If we look at the price history of gold since the bottom price in 1999, one might say that this new bull market has already begun. We know why the bull market should begin, and why it should unfold for a lengthy period of time, but the question that remains is, "How will it end?"

One way to answer this question is to look back at the great bull markets in gold that occurred in the past to see how they ended. We did this, and what we learned is that all of the great bull markets in gold have ended with a climactic event that is often called a gold rush. We also found a very important fact related to the ebb and flow of gold prices and interest in gold over the years. That fact is this: *There is a forty-year cycle in gold prices.*

How do we know this? That is a great question, especially since gold has only been traded freely in the United States since the early 1970s. Because of this limited duration of trading, we have not even seen unrestricted gold trading for long enough to infer a cycle of that length. Until the U.S. severed the 1944 Bretton Woods

Agreement in 1971, the U.S. dollar was tied to gold so that the price of gold was set and controlled by the U.S. Treasury Department; free trading of gold did not begin until 1975. Inferring a forty-year cycle from price data which does not even stretch back for that amount of time is quite a difficult task. So how do we know about this forty-year cycle?

We infer it from the public's reaction to gold, in a psychological sense, and from the behavior of governments with respect to gold. Perhaps we should refine our topic sentence as follows: *There is a forty-year cycle in gold rushes.*

What is a gold rush? Well, it is not is a geological phenomenon. Gold is discovered in new places all the time, but it takes a critical psychological component to turn a gold discovery into a gold rush.

Our research has uncovered gold rushes about every forty years going all the way back to the 1500s. A study of each of these gold rushes and their sequence in history is an important step toward understanding when the next one is coming, and we are certain that another one is coming. Here is a review of the gold rushes of the past 400+ years.

In 1533, Pizarro seized the Inca Empire, initiating the New World gold rush, following on the heels of Cortez's conquering of the Aztecs in 1520. The governments of Spain and Portugal rushed to establish colonies in the Americas in the pursuit of these riches, and to a lesser extent other European countries did, too.

In 1560, no gold rush is recorded in the history books, partly due to depletion of existing mines and lack of the requisite economic backdrop.

In 1607, the Jamestown Colony was established to search for (rumored, but nonexistent) gold in Virginia. Backers of this expedition had to persuade investors to come up with the funds to hire a ship and crew and to recruit workers to immigrate to the New World. They also had to equip them for the journey and the anticipated expedition in search of gold. It was quite a speculation, especially without evidence of the actual existence of gold in Virginia aside from just rumors and stories. The fact that they did not find gold does not change the fact that the human behavior involved with this movement was the sign of a gold rush. Remember that we are talking about a psychological event, not a mineral one. The backers and the participants in this expedition were so willing to take on the risks inherent with the mission in exchange for the prospect of finding gold that they suspended reasoned thought and risked life, limb, and capital in a fruitless effort. They must have had some serious feelings about the value of gold in order to take such a risk, feelings borne of hard economic times. The 1640s saw complex gold and silver mining activities in Central and South America, difficult to pinpoint as a classic gold rush.

From 1686 to 1691 there was a doubling of gold and silver deposits into the Bank of Amsterdam, following forty years of stagnation. In England the economic disruption of the 1680s led to the Glorious Revolution of 1688, when the Protestant William of Orange landed in Britain on November 5, 1688. (He was the William for whom the College of William and Mary in Virginia was named. His arrival caused the catholic King James to flee London, dumping the Great Seal of the realm in the Thames as he fled.)

In 1694 the Bank of England was established, taking over the role previously held by goldsmiths of issuing gold-backed notes as the "currency" of England. This episode of a government takeover of a gold/currency market will be repeated in the future. It is important to reflect on the significance in the history of gold because it brought about a fundamental change in the relationship of gold and paper money to the economy of the time. Prior to the creation of the Bank of England, merchants and traders who had excess gold would put it on deposit with a goldsmith in exchange for a promissory note for that amount of gold upon demand. These notes became a form of tender, tradable among merchants and much easier to transport than actual gold. In a word, the notes were currency, and backed by gold, which is more than we can say lately.

Goldsmiths, being shrewd businessmen, realized that they could make a nice profit by loaning out more promissory notes than they had gold on hand to back them, since it was unlikely that they would all be claimed at once. The new government of King William saw that this was far too lucrative a power to be left in the hands of private "banks," and so the creation of the Bank of England effectively nationalized the business of changing gold for paper notes. King William also required an efficient means to raise money for the governmental expansions he needed, including improving the armed forces.

Governments tend to be ponderous organizations that are slow to realize the changes taking place around them. So the recognition by the government of England that gold had exceptional value was a sign of the times and was the functional equivalent of a gold rush. This move to establish the Bank of England also helped to solidify the origins of the forty-/eighty-year cycle in gold rushes which still affects us today.

This gold rush also did not solve all of the festering economic problems of that period, problems which led to an economic war from 1701 to 1714 known as the War of the Spanish Succession.

From 1703 to 1720 Brazil saw a big gold boom. According to Pierre Vilar in *A History of Gold and Money* there was a large Portuguese emigration to Brazil for the gold mining industry, which included people from every walk of life. Even priests who were sent to the colonies got caught up in the gold mining fever. "The stampede of priests became a scandal," Vilar writes. Attempts were made to forbid them from going near the mines. The Governor of Sao Paolo went so far as to ask for permission to apply excommunication as a sanction to maintain the ban. In 1720 Portugal had to impose a strict limitation on emigration.

In 1768 there was a silver rush in Mexico. This was fueled by two factors: the economic weakness in the new world following the French and Indian War, and the discovery of silver by Obregón that led to the establishment of La Valenciana Mining Company. That led to an emigration of coal miners from Wales, and tin miners from Cornwall, both groups being available and desperate for work because of an economic slowdown in Britain. Other workers came from the English colonies in what is now the United States and Canada. Silver production in Mexico doubled over the next ten years. But that rush and its eventual economic collapse were associated with economic dissatisfaction throughout the New World (concerning the whole colonialist structure) and contributed to the economic movements which culminated in the Revolutionary War in 1776.

In 1799, gold was discovered by farmer John Reed, a Hessian deserter from the Revolutionary War, who had settled in North Carolina. Reed discovered a seventeen-pound gold nugget on his farm. Actually, it was his son who discovered the nugget, as John Reed and his wife already rode off to church that day on their one horse, while his son was bow-hunting in or along Little Meadow Creek for fish. The arrow struck the big nugget in the creek, and the youth brought the shiny rock home. The family used the big yellow rock as a fancy doorstop in their home for three years, and it was not until 1802 that Reed's wife suggested he take that shiny rock to town and see what he might get for selling it.

A Fayetteville jeweler gave Reed $3.50 for the nugget, which was worth thousands at the time and would be worth $71,000 today (given a gold price of $350/oz.). The amusing part of the story does not end there. Reed considered the $3.50 in hard currency a worthwhile sum at the time for just a shiny rock, and decided to splurge a bit and spend part of the windfall to purchase some strange brown beans, the likes of which he had never seen before. He brought them home for his wife, reasoning that they would make a fine pot of beans when boiled with salt pork.

On his way home, Reed told his in-laws of his good fortune, and they searched the area for more of the yellow metal, which they were able to find in some quantity. Reed reasoned that it would be a welcome source of income to collect and sell these shiny rocks after he got the crops laid in. But word got around Fayetteville about the jeweler's cheating of this poor farmer out of valuable gold, and Reed soon learned that the big rock was worth more than the $3.50 he was paid. To add insult to injury, the meal his wife had prepared with the special beans was disliked by the whole family; the coffee beans that he had bought were so bitter that no one could eat them.

Reed eventually came to terms of settlement of his case with the jeweler, and went on to reap even bigger riches by receiving a share of the gold that was dug out of his farm and creek. Word of the find set off a large migration to North Carolina beginning in 1802 to dig for gold in the area around Reed's farm.

That chapter of gold's history was one of the darkest. The quest for gold in the Carolinas and in Georgia led to the eviction of the whole Cherokee tribe from gold-bearing lands they held by tradition and by treaty in Georgia. They were forced to march along the "Trail of Tears" to Indian Territory (present day Oklahoma) in 1838 so that Cherokee lands could be seized for the purposes of gold mining.

The depression which followed this gold rush was made worse by an English blockade of U.S. ports, and helped push public sentiment to the point where Congress decided it would be a good idea to go to war again with England, this time in the War of 1812. So just as we saw the creation of the Bank of England being followed by the War of Spanish Succession, and the Mexican silver boom preceding the Revolutionary War, an economic war (the War of 1812) came in the wake of a gold rush.

In 1848, 46 years after the beginning of the Carolina gold rush, James Marshall was credited with discovering gold at Sutter's Mill on the American River near Sacramento, California. That set off the great gold rush, and led to the nickname of "49ers" to describe those who came to California in the great migration which followed that discovery. Interestingly, James Marshall died drunk and destitute, never striking it big in terms of gold mining, and living off the proceeds from the sale of his signature on collector cards.

Prospectors by the tens of thousands abandoned their jobs, homes, and families in the east to migrate across the entire continent, merely for the opportunity to use a pick and pan to try and "strike it rich." The odds against success in these endeavors were astronomical, although most people ignored that at the time. And the odds of surviving the voyage to get there were not so good either. Prospectors had to endure either a 2,000-mile walk across prairie, mountain, and desert, all before trails were very well marked, and with "dangerous savages" said to be lurking behind every rock and bush. Another choice was to sail (at great expense) from eastern ports, around the southern tip of South America, and then to San Francisco, only to have still farther to go on foot after arrival. Some also sailed to the Isthmus of Panama (then part of the country of Colombia), made an overland passage from Atlantic to Pacific (fighting mosquitoes, disease, etc.), and then caught another ship to California. To contemplate such a voyage by any of these routes and conclude it would be a worthwhile idea required that a person have a particular attitude about the relative value of gold in comparison to the value of an individual's current status quo. It takes several years of economic hard times to bring a large number of people to hold that sort of attitude.

The crash which followed this gold rush came in October 1857, after the September 12, 1857 sinking of the S.S. Central America with its large cargo of gold bullion and coins off the coast of the Carolinas. The impact was a dramatic interruption of monetary liquidity, as debts which were intended to be paid with that gold went unpaid; insurance companies failed and asset prices crashed. The loss of so much gold in this sinking increased the impetus to build the transcontinental railroad, but more important, the economic troubles that were the backdrop for the gold rush were exacerbated; this cataclysmic event fueled the buildup in public sentiment that resulted in the Civil War.

The same sort of economic weakness which prevailed during the 1840s showed itself again in the 1880s as the United States tried to grapple with the conversion from the postwar currency troubles of the 1860s and 1870s. To help finance the buildup for the Civil War, the U.S. made a temporary issuance of legal tender notices which were not backed in specie; unwinding that issuance was a difficult task, since there were two forms of currency circulating, and the U.S. could not long survive and prosper with two conflicting types of currency at once. The Treasury Department eventually came to a resolution of this problem, but not without consequence; several small panics in the 1870s and 1880s and a rise of labor activism (typified by the Haymarket Riots) marked the economic dissatisfaction of the type which presages all gold rushes.

In 1893, gold was discovered in the Klondike region of Alaska. People sold their belongings and enlisted the support of friends and relatives to help pay for not only the passage to Alaska, but also the necessary equipment required of new arrivals for expeditions into the Yukon. They did this simply on the speculation that the adventurer might have the opportunity to seek the gold which was reported to be there. Abandoning businesses, jobs, farms, and other sources of normal income in pursuit of the possibility of striking it rich seemed quite a rational idea at the time, as was selling assets to finance the expeditions of others, usually friends and family members.

As is the case with most gold rushes, few realized the gains they hoped for, and most fled back home busted and discouraged. The resulting depression throughout the 1890s led to excessive speculation and to financial panics in 1903 and 1907. Those panics fueled the call for the establishment of the Federal Reserve in 1913, and brought about the poor worldwide economic conditions which led to World War I.

The Great Depression of the early 1930s was a terrible example of monetary and economic collapse, not to mention political collapse for Herbert Hoover. With all of the problems the nation faced, Hoover had no chance to win reelection versus Franklin Roosevelt's challenge. Roosevelt took office in March 1933, and immediately set to work on "reforms." On January 31, 1934, the Gold Reserve Act went into effect forbidding households, banks, and businesses from holding more than a trivial amount of gold. Gold coins were rounded up by the government under force of law and melted down into gold ingots, which is why they are so rare today. This was used as a means of getting more paper money into circulation, and was quite an effective ploy although it proves that under the right conditions, the government can do things previously unimaginable.

In early 1934, President Roosevelt raised the official mint price of gold from $20.67 per ounce to $35 per ounce as a means of devaluing the dollar in comparison to gold. This set off a mini-gold rush among the Depression Era unemployed, who dragged out the pans and picks which their uncles and fathers had used in the previous century and set about prospecting for gold. Instantaneously, gold mines which had been unprofitable at $20.67 per ounce were suddenly quite profitable at $35 an ounce and were put back into operation. But the rebound effect of this gold rush resulted in an economic depression in 1937, and set into motion the economic forces which led to World War II.

In 1971, amid mounting pressure on the U.S. gold fixed at $35 per ounce, President Nixon announced that the U.S. was removing the gold backing from the dollar. Efforts to stimulate the economy during the 1960s had put so much pressure on the currency that it became impossible to maintain the gold fix in the international markets. This led eventually to the free trading of gold in cash markets by 1975, and in 1979 to 1980, a major gold rally took gold prices up as high as $850 and ounce in January of 1980. But that rally did not occur in a vacuum; it came on the heels of a decade of economic dissatisfaction brought about by a quagmire war in Vietnam, the Arab oil embargo, a presidential resignation in lieu of impeachment, the sexual revolution, the gender gap, and runaway inflation.

During this gold rush, there was some movement by individuals to take up the traditional gold rush activities of prospecting and panning for gold, but the big speculating that occurred during this gold rush came in the form of investors pursuing different forms of investing in gold and in the companies which mined it. Several newsletters touting gold stocks sprouted up, and investors flocked to various conventions and conferences where they could learn about the latest finds and opportunities to invest in "groundbreaking discoveries." The biggest of these conferences was the "Gold Show," which was also known as the Investments in Mining Conference. But that spike in gold prices was short-lived, and following the top in September 1980, gold prices entered a 21-year bear market to the twin bottoms in 1999 and 2001.

Following the big gold rush of the 1970s, the U.S. did not experience a big economic "shooting" war, although we did see the climax of the Cold War ("Mr. Gorbachev, tear down this wall!"). The Cold War may not have originated as an economic conflict, but its resolution was certainly borne from economic muscle. The U.S. outspent the Soviet Union on defense, leading the decaying economic and political structures (which held that empire together) to weaken beyond repair, and resulted in the breakup of the Soviet Union into its independent republics.

To summarize, there have been identifiable gold rushes in recorded history back into the 1500s, and the U.S. has seen gold rushes about every forty years, beginning with the 1768 Mexico Silver Rush, the 1802 North Carolina Gold Rush, the 1849 California Gold Rush, the 1893 Klondike Gold Rush, the 1934 mini gold rush, and the 1971-80 gold rush.

Why is it important to understand this rhythm? Because the forty-year cycle tells us that the next gold rush is due sometime in the 2010s. As we have seen from the past examples, there will need to be a decade or so of economic dissatisfaction and problems in order to set the stage for the next gold rush. People will need to be led by economic events to the point of believing that giving up all that they have in exchange for the opportunity to try to find gold, or to speculate on the possibility of gold prices rising, is actually a good idea.

Can you imagine people of today deciding to sell all that they own in order to travel halfway around the world to some godforsaken place just for the chance to dig for gold and hope to find some? Such a thought would be ridiculous, because right now there are far too many other opportunities to available. It will take a protracted period of economic weakness to foster the right type of mentality in the public that can bring about the next gold rush.

An important point to remember about gold rushes is that they are fairly brief events, lasting only a few years from initiation until climax. The California Gold Rush began in 1848 or 1849, and peaked in 1854. The Klondike Gold Rush peaked in 1898, also less than five years from its inception. The late 1970s gold rally began from a bottom in August 1976 and ended with the price top in September 1980. But during the lead up to the climax of a gold rush, gold must go through certain steps which result in its publicly perceived value to be increasing, setting up the conditions under which people are willing to go to extraordinary extremes to go out and find it.

Gold must first be considered as having lost its value. We witnessed that in 1999 and 2000 as several countries' central banks decided to sell off their gold holdings, since those assets were perceived as not worth holding. We also saw a decrease in the fascination with gold among members of the public. The aforementioned

Investments in Mining Conference actually changed its name in 2000 to "The New Opportunities Conference," since the organizers reasoned that they were going to have trouble drawing a crowd to a trade show about precious metals, and they wanted to broaden the appeal. That told us at the time that we were witnessing a generational bottom in gold prices for this cycle.

After gold is considered an unworthy investment, the next step in the progression toward a gold rush is a general rise in gold prices over several years which should help to set the stage for people to believe that gold is once again a better place for their attention rather than tech stocks, dividends, real estate, lottery tickets, their jobs, their families, and just about everything else of importance. That should be accomplished just before the big gold rush which is due in the late 2010s. Almost no one is at that stage now, and it will take some work to reach that stage.

In this chapter, we have clearly laid out the time sequence of the various gold rushes that can be identified in history, and they all share an interval of about forty to forty-five years. When we have presented this topic to the public in past lectures; one of the questions that often arises is whether the advancements in technology will bring a truncation in this long cycle. This is an excellent question, since we have seen some changes in some very short-term stock market cycles brought on by the advent of day-trading, discount brokerage fees, and the change from a five-day settlement to a three-day settlement. But we have also seen that the longer stock market cycles, specifically the important nine-month cycle and four-year presidential cycle, have remained in effect with their same periodicities before and after these developments.

This suggests that the periodicies of these longer cycles are not sensitive to changes in the "viscosity" of money, but rather to some unknown human behavioral cycle. The nine-month cycle happens to coincide with the human gestation period, which may just be a coincidence.

As to the question of technology, in all of the history of gold rushes we have continually had technological changes which have sped up the economy. Clipper ships, steam ships, telegraphs, railroads, radios, etc. have all been developed to speed the flow of information, and yet the long cycle in gold is still about forty years in length. One may think that there has never been a technology revolution to the extent of the Internet, but just think for a moment about the difference between a horse and buggy versus a railroad; which do you think has made the bigger difference to the people of the times?

One of the important aspects of gold rushes that is critical to their development is that no one can be around who remembers the last one, and who can therefore explain to the young whippersnappers that it might not be a good idea to head off into the Arctic Circle to hunt for gold, and that gold prices can, in fact, go down as well as up. Throughout history, people have had both a working and an investing life of about forty years, so it takes about forty years for the last of the previous gold rush's participants to die off; that may be the controlling factor for this long cycle. One might think that with the medical developments that have allowed people to live longer, there might still be some people around in the 2010s who remember the 1979 to 1980 gold rush climax. But do you think that Generation Y is going listen to the stories of those "old fogies"? After all, it's different this time…

The last point to remember about gold rushes is that they mark the end of the bull market in gold, not the beginning of it. Gold prices tend to make long, boring bottom patterns on price charts and then make fast, climactic tops. This is true in every time frame we have studied, from five-minute bar charts all the way up to monthly charts. A gold rush, therefore, is the climactic concluding event that ends a long gold bull market, although almost no one realizes it nor wants to accept it at the time, just as everything is going so well and gold prices are "surely" headed to $5,000 or even $10,000 an ounce.

But when you see the signs of a gold rush building in the 2010s, with people touting a great new technology for gold panning equipment and hot new discoveries in some strange, exotic, and steamy part of the world, you will recognize that as the sign that the party is about to be over. And you can swear to yourself that you will be sure to tell your grandchildren about the great gold boom of the 2000s and 2010s, and how to recognize the signs of their own gold rush forty years hence. You can also prepare yourself for the economic war of the 2020s which will surely follow this gold rush.

Chapter 9
What to Buy, What to Avoid

There are literally dozens of different forms of physical gold bullion on the market, an assortment of coins and bars in all sorts of weights, shapes, and sizes produced by dozens of countries and private mints around the world. In this chapter we'll examine some of the most popular forms of bullion coins to give you some idea as to what's available on the market.

Say NO to Gold Bars!

I love those gold bars you see in the movies. Stacks of 100-ounce bars are commonly the targets of thieves and villains. 100-ounce bars are primarily traded on the major world commodity exchanges and used by the world's central banks when trading gold.

Private investors, buying less than 1,000 ounces of gold, should steer clear of these 100-ounce gold bars. I strongly recommend <u>NEVER</u> buying smaller gold bars like one-ounce or less weighted gold bars produced by private mints or refiners.

First of all, small investors who buy one or two 100-ounce bars lose the ability to sell their gold in intelligent increments. If gold doubles as I suspect it will, it may make sense for an investor to sell 25%, to 50% of his gold holdings. 100-ounce bars make that very difficult. In addition, only exchanges regularly trade 100-ounce bars. Most gold dealers, coin dealers, and gold brokers don't trade 100-ounce bars and will discount a bar that large by 5% to 7%. OUCH!

Second, the marketplace is dominated by bullion coins. The vast majority of rare coin and bullion dealers do 99% of their trading in coin form. My personal experience with gold bars has been consistently bad. They sell for a 3% to 10% premium over the spot price of gold and when you sell them you get back –3% to –10% less than the spot price of gold. That works out to a spread of as much as 20%, which is way too big of a buy/sell spread on bullion gold coins. It's important here to make a distinction between bullion coins and numismatic coins. A *bullion* coin's value is derived solely from the content of its gold and is normally sold at a small premium above the market price for gold. A *numismatic* coin derives its value from its rarity, historical and aesthetic qualities and can sell for up to a million dollars. I will discuss rare coins in the next chapter.

Say NO to Private Mint Gold Coins!

Now that I've steered you away from gold bullion bars let me also caution you against private mint gold coins. Many refiners and private mints around the world produce one-ounce to 1/10-ounce gold coins and offer them for sale as "bullion" alternatives. They tout either the fact that they cost less than more commonly traded gold bullion coins produced by the governments of United States, Canada, South Africa and Australia, or that they are sold based on the uniqueness of their design. Private mints coin their gold bullion with images of everything from sporting events to Elvis Presley. You should never buy privately minted gold bullion coins. They sell for large premiums above the price of gold and sell at a discount to their intrinsic gold value because they are NOT widely bought and sold by dealers and therefore dealers will discount the coins when (or if) they buy them.

So, what gold bullion coins can you buy safely for a modest premium?

Stick With the Five Most Commonly Traded Gold Bullion Coins in the World!

Back in the 1970s the most famous gold bullion unit was the Krugerrand from South Africa. The coins contain one ounce of gold and just enough copper to allow the coin to be struck. So the net weight of the coin is actually more than an ounce. They dominated trading in the last gold bull market and are still traded today. The South African government produces small-weighted coins in addition to the one-ounce standard.

South African Krugerrand
No currency value
Gross weight: 33.933 grams (1.0909 troy ounces)
Fineness: .916 or 22 karats
Diameter: 34mm
Also available in: 1/2, 1/4, 1/10-ounce coins

The popularity of the South African Krugerrand prompted the Canadian government to mint the Canadian Maple Leaf in 1979. The coin was an instant success thanks to a clever advertising angle that touted the Canadian Maple Leaf as the first solid 24-karat gold bullion coin. While that is true, the fact remains that Canadian and South African coins both contain one full troy ounce of gold. Few people realize that the Canadian Maple Leaf actually has a face value of $50 Canadian dollars, far less of course than the value of the gold bullion.

Canadian Maple Leaf
Face value: $50 Canadian
Gross weight: 33.1033 grams (1 troy ounces)
Fineness: .999 or 24 karats
Diameter: 30mm
Also available in: 1/2, 1/4, 1/10-ounce coins

The "Roo," as it's commonly called, is minted by the Australian Perth Mint and is actually the second bullion coin produced by Australia. The first was called the "Nugget Coin" and the Kangaroo replaced it.

Australian Kangaroo
Face value: $100 Australian
Gross weight: 31.1033 grams (1 troy ounces)
Fineness .999 or 24 karats
Diameter: 32.10mm
Also available in: 1/2, 1/4, 1/10-ounce coins

One of the most popular gold bullion coins the world is the China Panda, which was first introduced in 1982. The 1/20-ounce was introduced in 1983. Throughout the years, the China Mint has kept the same Panda design but has frequently changed the position of the Panda on its coins.

Panda
Face value: 500 Rinimbi/Yuan
Gross weight: 32.05 grams (1.0909 troy ounces)
Fineness: .999 or 24 karats
Diameter: 32.5 mm
Also available in: 1/2, 1/4, 1/10, 1/20-ounce coins

The American Gold Eagle is now by far the most popular gold bullion coin in the world. Authorized by Congress in 1985 and first minted in 1986, American Eagles are minted in 22-karat which was the standard established for circulating U.S. gold, dating back to gold that was first struck in 1796. In fact the 22-karat standard has been the worldwide standard for circulating gold coinage for more than 350 years!

American Gold Eagles have a substantial patriotic edge as they can only be coined from newly mined sources in the United States. The balance of the coin's composition consists of silver and copper, which is added to increase the coin's durability. Gold is a very soft metal.

The obverse is based on world-renowned American sculptor Augustus Saint-Gauden's design for the prized 1907 $20 gold coin. The reverse pictures a family of eagles symbolizing family tradition and unity.

Which gold bullion coin do I recommend? Hands down the best gold bullion coin is the American Gold Eagle! It's the most liquid coin in the world. The buy/sell spread is rarely more than 7% on small amounts and as little as 5% on quantities.

American Eagle
Face value: $50
Gross weight: 39.33 grams (1.0910 troy ounces)
Fineness: .916 or 22 karats
Diameter: 32.7 mm
Fine gold content: 31.103 grams (1 troy ounce)
Also available in: 1/2, 1/4, 1/10, 1/20-ounce coins

Important Things to Keep in Mind When Buying Any Gold Bullion Coins

Don't buy bullion coins that have any rim nicks, scratches, abrasions, chips, or dents or those that appear to be discolored in any way. NEVER! Any knowledgeable buyer will discount coins that have even the slightest damage.

Steer clear of any coins that have carbon or copper spots. Some gold bullion coins, even those that are in 100% absolutely perfect condition will have tiny spots visible to the naked eye without magnification. These are natural and caused by the inclusion of copper in the gold to increase the durability of the planchets (the metal disks) on which the coins are struck. Despite the fact that these spots are natural to gold coins they are undesirable, and dealers will buy and sell them at a small discount. Make sure when buying gold bullion coins you insist on "no spots." Keep in mind a spot is only a problem if you can see it with the naked eye. If you have to use a magnifying glass to see a spot it is not a problem.

Don't buy "rare date" bullion coins. A bullion coin is a bullion coin. Don't be fooled. The least expensive way to purchase the one-ounce coin is to specify "common date." Common date means the bullion dealer can send you any date bullion coins of the type you desire in Gem condition. If you order a specific date, for example 1996, it will cost more then the common date.

Some telemarketing firms are now selling some dates of the American Eagle one-ounce gold coins in Mint State condition for premiums of 10%, 20% even 30%! Yuck — what a horrible deal. It's a complete rip-off. The coins are and will always be bullion coins. They're NOT rare and don't deserve a premium.

NEVER buy or sell gold bullion strictly on the basis of the best price. Saving a few dollars with buying/selling prices versus dealing with a reputable company/person is silly. Over the years I've seen investors decide to do business with one dealer or another based 100% on price. The firm could offer the best price because they had no intention of delivering the gold! When the gold market gets red-hot, the scam artists breed like rats. Here are two recommendations I always make:

Know your dealer. Do some background checking. How long has the dealer been in business? Check with the Better Business Bureau. Are you dealing with a "nameless" clerk or a principal in the firm on whom you can check? You'd be amazed how many "colorful" people are out there waiting to steal your money.

Always take immediate delivery of your gold coins. NEVER store your gold coins in a dealer's vault. I've seen people lose every penny trusting a dealer. Take the time and get a safety deposit box at your bank and take charge of the storage. When buying bullion it's important to get your gold as quickly as possible. Checks need several days to clear, money orders need less time, and bank wires are immediate; you can always insist on next-day shipment when you send a bank wire.

When the Gold Market Gets Red-Hot!

I'm going to give it to you straight. When the gold market gets red-hot, and it will, EVERY gold dealer and precious metals brokerage firm will pay spot (most current price) for your gold coins and sell at 10% over spot. The bid/ask spread at which gold coins are traded will widen. It happened in 1979 and 1980 and it will happen again. Don't sweat it. Take your profits and don't let the wider premiums bother you.

The best analogies…

> **Gasoline:** When we experience a "shortage," gas stations gouge. It happens every time. A frenzied marketplace creates fear, which widens the spread and prices rise. Buyers get the short end of the stick while dealers get rich.

> **Stocks:** Forget all the nonsense about reform on Wall Street. The fact is when a stock becomes red-hot, the spread between the buy and sell widens. The specialists who run the market make much more money. They argue that the spread widens because the transaction risk increases. This isn't always true but it's true enough that they can get away with the wider buy/sell spread.

Bottom Line: Get into your gold investments now before the market gets red-hot. Diversify your investment portfolio because it's the smart thing to do. Get yourself into a position to ride gold from $350 to $1,250 or $2,000 an ounce. Buy the best, most liquid gold investments and cash in on the bull market ahead.

Chapter 10
Investing and Collecting United States Gold Coins: The Best Approach

I've been fascinated by rare gold coins ever since I was a child. They're truly magical to behold. While it is true that I collect and invest in rare gold coins from around the world I've been especially focused on pre-1933 United States gold coins. My fascination with U.S. gold coins was reinforced by two events when I was a teenager in the 1970s:

Event #1: The legalization of private gold ownership in 1973.

Event #2: The wild double-digit inflation of the 1970s.

When gold was legalized in 1973, many rare coin dealers quickly became gold bullion dealers as well. So many of the rare coin dealers with whom I traded suddenly became bullion dealers.

It became very clear to me (from watching the businesses of my dealer acquaintances) that while most gold investors gravitated towards buying bullion gold coins like Kruggerands, Maple Leafs, and gold bars the better asset by far was investment-quality U.S. rare gold coins.

That observation back in the 1970s has proven true. Gem Uncirculated U.S. gold coins struck from 1796 through 1933 have consistently outperformed every bullion alternative for the past thirty-three years, without exception.

A "Gem Uncirculated" U.S. gold coin is a coin that remains in the original state of preservation; these quality coins look as they did on the day they were struck. A Gem quality coin may have a minor bag mark or an abrasion but for the most part a Gem coin's surfaces remain in a near-perfect state.

Rare coins are graded much like diamonds. Rare coin-grading uses a scale of 1 through 70. A coin graded 70 is considered perfect. The designation "MS" stands for Mint State. Coins in Mint State condition are graded MS-60 through MS-70.

It's virtually impossible to find an MS-70 gold coin from 1796 through 1933. Collectors prize Choice Uncirculated coins grading MS-64 and MS-65 and lust after Gem Uncirculated coins grading MS-66, MS-67, MS-68 and MS-69.

Gem quality gold coins from 1796 to 1933 are truly rare, as only a few survived. To understand this rarity, you have to keep in mind that these coins were minted as spending money. Precious few collectors had the disposable income to put aside gold coins as collectibles in the nineteenth century or in the early part of the twentieth century, much less through the Great Depression of the 1930s!

Because of their scarcity, Gem quality U.S. gold coins offer a genuine and unique *one-way leverage* that literally no other gold investment offers. This became evident to me back in the 1970s. As the price of gold steadily moved higher during the 1970s the price of Gem Uncirculated rare U.S. gold coins rose even faster, sometimes outpacing the rise in bullion by as much as two to one!

For example, a Gem Uncirculated MS-66 $20 gold Saint-Gaudens in 1974 went from being worth $175 to trading for more than $2,000 in 1980 at the peak of gold's rise. While gold bullion went from $145 to $850 an ounce, that Gem Uncirculated $20 Saint-Gaudens enjoyed more than two-to-one advantage in price appreciation!

This amazing leverage became even more spectacular when gold peaked and entered what became a twenty-two-year bear market. While the price of gold dropped, many rare Gem Uncirculated gold coins from 1796 to 1933 actually continued to increase in value.

In fact, if you had moved from gold bullion in 1980 to really Gem rare U.S. gold, and held the coins the past twenty-two years you would have actually made a substantial amount of money. Of course there are exceptions to this rule. But as a whole the Gem

Uncirculated rare U.S. Gold coins have consistently been big winners over bullion gold year in and year out. Here are a couple of typical examples:

- A Gem Uncirculated MS-66 1916-S $20 Saint Gaudens $20 gold coin in 1980 at the top of the gold market would have cost you no more than $2,000. Today, twenty-three years later, that very coin now trades wholesale for $5,750. A gain of 187% while the price of gold fell from $850 in 1980 to just $342 in 2003!

- A Gem Uncirculated MS-66 1929 $2.50 Indian gold coin in 1980 would have cost about $2,000 in 1980. Today, that same coin would trade wholesale between dealers for as much as $8,500. *A gain of 325% while gold has fallen more than 59%!*

This unique *one-way leverage* is the result of the growing numismatic interest in these coins, which supersedes the effects of a bearish gold market. This is true in large part because of the U.S. government's marketing efforts as mentioned in the next examples.

In the past twenty-two years the number of rare coin collectors coming into the market has vastly outnumbered the supply of these rare gold coins because of the marketing efforts of the U.S. Mint. Each year the U.S. Mint produces, promotes, and sells hundreds of thousands of U.S. Mint and proof sets, as well as seemingly never-ending series of modern commemorative, half, dollar, and $5 gold coins. The current U.S. Commemorative Quarter program is another amazing promotion program used by the mint to generate new coin collectors every day.

It's been estimated by industry experts that the U.S. Mint brings more than half a million new rare coin collectors into the hobby every year. Even if a small number of these new collectors decide to collect truly rare coins like 1796 to 1933 Gem Uncirculated U.S. gold coins, the price of these coins must rise substantially regardless of whether the price of gold goes up and down. Again this one-way leverage is amazing.

To put this in perspective: Only 96 Gem Uncirculated 1916-S $20 gold coins survive in Gem Uncirculated MS-66 condition. And only two 1929 $2.50 Gold Indians survive in Gem Uncirculated MS-66 condition.* If only 1% of these new collectors entering the market decide to collect these Gem Uncirculated gold coins, there will be 5,000 new buyers chasing these few coins. In the last 33 years this has produced a steady rise in the value of these coins. Can you imagine what the price gains will be in a new bull gold market? It's going to be explosive!

Having pointed out this unique one-way leverage of Gem Uncirculated Rare U.S. gold coins and the investment potential for them in a bullish gold market, let me add that this information is especially important now that we are at the threshold of a major new bull market in gold. While I've listed many of the reasons for a new bull market earlier in this book including monetary expansion, the falling value of the-dollar, global uncertainty and tension, potential for a financial crisis, and investor demand and shrinking supply, allow me to point out two precise macro-economic reasons that should motivate you to immediately start buying Gem Uncirculated 1796 to 1933 U.S. gold coins.

The U.S. dollar is tumbling in value: Much to the dismay of central bankers in Europe and Japan, the dollar is falling against the Euro and the yen. Nominal interest rates are now so low that government bond buyers are complacent. For the first time in a decade the "real" federal funds rate is negative (i.e., 1.25% funds rate minus the 2.4% year-over-year gains in December Consumer Price Index is a negative 1.15%). A falling dollar and a negative federal funds rate is for gold what kerosene is to fire.

Government printing presses are working overtime: Bernard S. Bernanke, one of America's foremost monetary economists and one of Alan Greenspan's new hires at the Federal Reserve Board, reminded a Washington audience in November that the Fed has a marvelous invention at its disposal for fighting deflation. The device is called a "printing press," said Bernanke; with

---

* *Graded by Professional Coin Grading Service (PCGS) and Numismatic Guarantee Corporation (NGC) on or before 8/21/03*

it the government can "produce as many U.S. dollars as it wishes, at essentially no cost."

This willingness to print money is not exclusively the privilege of the U.S. Federal Reserve. On January 9, 2003 an auction of ten-year Japanese government bonds was 18.6 times oversubscribed, although their coupon rate was only .09%. For perspective, Haruhhiko Kuroda, one of the top contenders to take over the governorship of the Bank of Japan, has pledged to print enough yen to push his nation's inflation rate to 3%.

Based on the continuing malaise of the Japanese economy and the struggling U.S. economy to avoid a double-dip recession, monetary expansion will continue to increase.

While the War in Iraq is largely over, the war on terrorism is a long way from a conclusion. As a result our military buildup is likely guaranteed through the next two decades. The last time our country embarked on waging a long war, not nearly as expensive at this war on terrorism, was in the 1960s. Back then our nation's politicians also tried cutting taxes, and that "guns and butter" policy sowed the seeds for the terrible inflation we suffered in the 1970s. If there is one constant throughout the history of mankind, it is the reckless economic policies of politicians. How many governments have fallen? How much misery have politicians caused with an open checkbook? Unfortunately, it has become a perpetually recurring story.

What to Know Before You Buy a Single Rare U.S. Gold Coin!

There are two independent and reliable grading and authentication services in the rare coin market. They are the Numismatic Guarantee Corporation (NGC) found online at www.ngccoin.com and Professional Coin Grading Service (PCGS) found online at www.pcgs.com. **NEVER** buy a rare coin that hasn't been graded and certified as authentic by one of these two services. **NEVER!** Both services ultrasonically seal the coins they grade and certify them in airtight plastic holders that protect the coin and make storage and resale easy.

There are a lot of rare coin grading services that attempt to imitate NGC and PCGS in the marketplace but they are NOT reliable. In my experience, rare dealers that try to sell coins not graded by either NGC or PCGS are less than ethical.

Both NGC and PCGS grade their coins based on the Sheldon scale that I described at the beginning of this chapter. I recommend both Choice and Gem Uncirculated MS-66 condition coins most often for two reasons. I think that many of the coins I love offer the best investment potential and simply are unavailable in Gem MS-66 condition. Sometimes the best possible coins are only available in Choice Uncirculated condition MS-65.

Building a Gem Uncirculated U.S. Gold Type Set

One of the best ways to position yourself and diversify your investment portfolio is to assemble a Gem Uncirculated 20th Century (pre-1933) U.S. Gold Type Set. Depending on your budget, there are several possible sets that can be assembled. The eight-piece type set is the most commonly assembled set for investors and it includes an example of all eight U.S. gold coins minted by the United States for circulation from 1900 through 1933.

An eight-piece 20th century gold set includes two examples of the $2.50, $5 and $10 gold coins, one each of the Liberty and Indian Types, and one example of each of the Liberty and Saint-Gaudens $20 gold coins.

In my opinion, assembling a Gem Uncirculated MS-66 eight-piece gold set graded and certified by either of the two most respected independent grading services (NGC or PCGS) is the single best gold physical investment an investor can make. The coins are legitimately rare and should offer as much as a three-to-one leverage in the unfolding bull market in gold ahead. Here's a brief run-down of the coin types that make up this eight-piece U.S. gold type set and the rarity and price you can expect to pay at this point in time.

Coin #1: Gold $2.50 Liberty (1840-1907)

The $2.50 Liberty Gold Coin was one of the backbones of America's monetary system for sixty-seven years. In many parts of the United States at that time, paper money was NEVER accepted as payment for goods and services. Merchants commonly insisted on payment in gold or silver. The Liberty Series was designed by Christian Gobrecht and actually outlived the famous sculptor by sixty years!

This long series is filled with terrific rarities, but there are numerous late dates that survived in remarkable condition. A nice supply of post-1900 Liberty $2.50 gold coins exist in Gem Uncirculated MS-66 examples, which have been graded by NGC or PCGS and now sell for about $2,200 each. These $2.50 Liberty Gold Coins were struck at five different U.S. Mints during the life of the series: Philadelphia (no mint mark), New Orleans (O located on the base of the reverse under the eagle), San Francisco (S located on the base of the reverse under the eagle), Charlotte (C located on the base of the reverse under the eagle) and Dahlonega (D located on the base of the reverse under the eagle).

I especially like some of the rare dates and lower population coins that you can buy for modest premiums. Rare dates will give you added upside and when completing a ten-piece gem uncirculated U.S. gold type set with better date coins you stand the chance of obtaining an extra premium for the entire set.

NGC and PCGS have graded a total of 3,386 $2.50 Liberty Gold Coins MS-66. Higher-quality coins are available; 405 have been graded MS-67 and twenty-five MS-68. MS-69 are extremely rare and MS-70 coins are non-existent. They trade for $45,000 when available.

The table below shows price projections for Gem Uncirculated MS-66 $2.50 Liberty Gold Coins based on the combination of higher gold prices and the growing number of collectors and investors. I've also included price projections for the high quality and rare MS-67 graded examples of these coins because they are available and represent a solid investment in gold.

The projected price of these gold coins at the following gold prices

	$340	**$450**	**$550**	**$675**	**$750**	**$1,000**
MS-66	$2,100	$4,500	$7,000	$10,000	$13,500	$17,500
MS-67	$4,950	$7,000	$10,000	$13,500	$16,500	$22,500

Coin #2: $2.50 Indian (1908-1929)

The $2.50 and $5 Indian gold pieces introduced the wonderfully beautiful incuse design to American numismatics. The word "incuse" is so obscure outside of numismatics that it doesn't appear in some dictionaries, but in coin terminology it means that the devices of the design are recessed rather than raised in relation to the fields. A close personal friend of President Theodore Roosevelt, Dr. William Sturgis Bigelow, got the idea for these incuse designed coins from some of the coins minted by the Egyptian Fourth Dynasty.

Bigelow obtained the go-ahead from Roosevelt to persuade the famous Boston sculptor Bela Lyon Pratt to submit models in this technique. Pratt's Native American Chieftain model remains unnamed, his tribe unknown. Roosevelt enthusiastically approved the designs and ordered Pratt's models sent to the Philadelphia Mint for translation into master dies. The coins were minted predominantly in Philadelphia but coins were also minted in Denver (D located left of the base on the reverse under the eagle) in 1911, 1914, and 1925.

The rarest coins in this $2.50 Indian gold series include the 1911-D, 1914, and 1914-D. Issues in MS-66 are VERY rare and expensive. The 1909, 1910, 1912, 1913, 1925-D, and 1929 dates are also rare and I believe are VERY undervalued in Gem Uncirculated MS-66 condition. NGC and PCGS have graded just 351 of these beautiful coins MS-66. The 1908, 1925, 1926, 1927, and 1928 examples of these coins considered are still rare but can be bought in MS-66 condition for about $7,500 at the present time. MS-67 and better coins are GREAT rarities, seldom offered on the rare coin market.

The table below shows price projections for Gem Uncirculated MS-66 $2.50 Indian Gold coins based on the combination of higher gold prices and the growing number of collectors and investors. Please note that I am also including the current pricing of Choice Uncirculated MS-65 examples of this series and denomination because I believe they also possess great potential, and finding a MS-66 example may be very difficult. To date NGC and PCGS have graded just 3,637 coins MS-65.

The projected price of these gold coins at the following gold prices

	$340	$450	$550	$675	$750	$1,000
MS-65	$3,000	$4,000	$7,500	$11,000	$15,500	$21,500
MS-66	$6,750	$10,500	$14,000	$17,500	$22,500	$32,500

Coin #3: $5 Liberty, Motto (1866-1908)

The Congressional Act of March 3, 1865 which authorized the coinage of shield nickels and issue of certain classes of interest bearing notes, also ordered that henceforth all U.S. coins large enough to provide room must include the motto "IN GOD WE TRUST." The U.S. Mint took this to mean the Half Eagle, Eagle, and Double Eagle ($5, $10 and $20) U.S. Gold Coins. A "no motto" version of these $5.00 Liberty Gold Coins was struck from 1839 through 1866. But for the purpose of discussion, we will reference the more common but still rare "motto" type.

On April 15, 1933 just one month after his March 4th inauguration, President Franklin Roosevelt signed an executive order that made gold ownership illegal which required citizens to surrender "all old coin, gold bullion and old certificates by May 1, 1933." Exempt were true numismatic coins at the time, which Liberty $5.00 were NOT considered. So during the gold recall of 1933, huge quantities of $5 Liberty gold coins were shipped to Europe by hoarders in order to evade this order. In the 1970s many of these coins made their way back to the United States and were purchased by collectors. Swiss banks sold as many as 22,000 pieces in one gigantic sale. Not surprisingly, few coins survive in Gem Uncirculated condition.

NGC or PCGS Gem Uncirculated MS-66 examples now sell for about $5,000. These $5.00 Liberty gold coins were struck at five different U.S. Mints during the life of the series: Philadelphia (no mint mark), New Orleans (O located on the base of the reverse under the eagle), San Francisco (S located on the base of the reverse under the eagle), Charlotte (C located on the base of the reverse under the eagle) and Dahlonega (D located on the base of the reverse under the eagle). The coins struck from 1900 through 1908 were struck at just Philadelphia, San Francisco, and Denver Mints.

There's one neat variety of coin I love: the 1901-S/O. The "S" mint mark actually stands over an "O" mint mark on the reverse of the coin under the eagle. There are just a few MS-66 examples of this coin. Only one graded by NGC and one graded by PCGS as I write. They're probably worth $9,500 to $10,500 apiece. Of the balance of the coins in this 1900 to 1908 period, NGC and PCGS have graded just 556 coins MS-66!

These coins can be acquired in MS-67 condition, but are EXTREMELY rare in MS-68 and MS-69 condition.

Here are my price projections for Gem Uncirculated MS-66 $5.00 Liberty Gold coins:

The projected price of these gold coins at the following gold prices

	$340	$450	$550	$675	$750	$1,000
MS-66	$5,000	$8,250	$11,500	$15,500	$20,500	$29,500

Coin #4: $5 Indian (1908-1929)

The $5.00 Indian series has the same genesis as the $2.50 gold coins discussed earlier in this chapter. However this series is MUCH rarer, especially in MS-66 condition. In fact they are so rare that I make an exception with these coins as the $2.50 Indian Gold Coins and recommend them both Gem Uncirculated MS-66 and Choice Uncirculated MS-65 condition. The incuse design made it very difficult for Choice or Gem Coins to survive. These coins are most often available from rare coin dealers and at auction in Brilliant and Select Uncirculated condition (MS-60 through MS-63 grades), and still trade at substantial prices.

NGC and PCGS have graded less than 1,000 coins in MS-65 condition and just seventy-five coins in MS-66 condition. There are many rare dates, and they can trade for extremely high prices. A 1915-S in MS-65 recently traded hands for over $70,000. A 1911-D traded hands for $125,000!

I recommend the acquisition of any 1908, 1909, 1909-D, 1911, 1912, 1913, 1914, or 1915 in MS-65 or MS-66 condition. MS-67 and better coins are GREAT rarities that are seldom offered on the rare coin market.

These coins were struck at the Philadelphia, Denver, and San Francisco Mints and struck for only one year at the New Orleans Mint in 1909. This is the great rarity of the series and worth more than $200,000 in MS-66 and $350,000 in MS-66 condition!

Price projections for Choice Uncirculated MS-65 and Gem Uncirculated MS-66 condition $5.00 Indian Gold Coins struck from 1908-1929 are based on the combination of higher gold prices and growing number of collectors and investors.

The projected price of these gold coins at the following gold prices

	$340	**$450**	**$550**	**$675**	**$750**	**$1,000**
MS-65	$10,000	$14,000	$21,500	$29,500	$39,500	$57,500
MS-66	$17,500	$24,500	$32,500	$45,000	$62,500	$110,000

Coin #5: $10 Liberty, Motto (1866-1907)

The Liberty $10 Gold Coin has the same origins of its $5.00 cousins, with one big difference. These coins are much harder to find in Gem condition. The larger surfaces of this larger coin were more susceptible to scratches and abrasions, so there are far fewer coins grading MS-66 by either PCGS or NGC. Also adding to this problem is the higher denomination. Again, who had $10 to put away and save? Ten dollars was a great deal of money back at the turn of the century. Collectors who had money tended to hoard lower-denomination coins like $2.50 gold which explains why NGC and PCGS has graded 3,386 $2.50 coins in MS-66 and only 480 $10.00 gold coins.

Fortunately there have been a few small hoards of these beautiful coins uncovered over the past thirty years, approximately 1,000 that grade MS-65. Nearly 700 of those coins are dated 1901 or 1901-S. If it weren't for these hoarded dates, you'd be paying about $12,500 for MS-65 examples instead of $3,250. Gem quality MS-66 pieces are very scarce and sell for about $5,750 when available. I recommend MS-66 coins but also like the upside potential of Choice Uncirculated MS-65 coins. These coins were also struck in Denver, San Francisco, and Philadelphia Mints from 1900 through 1907. MS-67 grade coins are EXTREMELY RARE. As for higher quality coins, as they say in Brooklyn, "Forget about it!"

Price projections for Choice Uncirculated MS-65 and Gem Uncirculated MS-66 condition $10.00 Liberty Gold coins struck from 1900-1908 follow.

The projected price of these gold coins at the following gold prices

	$340	$450	$550	$675	$750	$1,000
MS-65	$3,000	$5,000	$7,500	$10,000	$14,500	$18,500
MS-66	$5,750	$9.250	$13,000	$16,500	$20,500	$32,500

Coin #6: $10 Indian (1907-1933) "Eagle"

Don't tell my wife, but I've had a love affair with this coin my entire life. While there are legitimate arguments among collectors about the best U.S. rare coin design over the past 227 years, I have always thought the Indian $10 design was the most beautiful. I certainly think it is one of the most undervalued and as a result has potentially the greatest upside potential. These $10 Indians come in two types: with motto and without. For the purposes of an eight-piece gold type set, either type would fit the bill.

There is one "hoard" date. The 1932 issue makes up more than 50% of the coins that survive in Choice Uncirculated MS-65 condition. Yet even the 1932 is really rare in Gem Uncirculated. The

$10 Indian was designed by one of the most America's famous sculptors, Augustus Saint-Gaudens, and was designed along with the $2.50, $5.00 and $20.00 gold designs requested by Teddy Roosevelt. The Native American Indian woman bears of all things, a feathered war bonnet. History tells us that no Indian woman would have ever worn such a headdress. The Eagle that adorns the reverse of these coins is reminiscent of the breathtaking sculptures of eagles that decorated both early Egyptian and Roman coins and buildings. The edge of the coins minted from 1907-1911 features forty-six stars, representing the states in the union at the time of its design. In 1912 two more stars were added in honor of two additional states, New Mexico and Arizona.

NGC and PCGS have graded altogether 3,439 motto and no-Motto $10 Indians in Choice Uncirculated MS and only 610 in Gem Unciruclated MS-66 condition. These coins are VERY rare in Gem MS-67 and MS-68 condition and are virtually impossible to locate in MS-69. I do not recommend buying the 1932 dated coins in anything less than MS-66 condition. The next most common coin is the 1926, which is a superb coin to buy MS-66 if you can. There are many key dates in this series. These $10 Indians were struck at just three mints: Philadelphia, Denver, and San Francisco.

If you have the disposable income/investment dollars please accept my invitation to build a complete set of these coins with my assistance. I've been working on a complete set for many years and can share important information most dealers would never share, and that few actually know. A type set Gem Uncirculated MS-66 can be acquired for about $5,500.

The projected price of these gold coins at the following gold prices

	$340	$450	$550	$675	$750	$1,000
MS-65	$3,300	$4,500	$7,500	$10,000	$14,500	$18,500
MS-66	$5,500	$9,750	$13,750	$18,500	$22,500	$35,000

Coin #7: $20 Liberty (1849-1907) "Double Eagle"

In 1849 Congress authorized the minting of the largest regularly-circulated gold coins the United States would have. These wonderful gold coins were struck at five U.S. Mints: Philadelphia, Denver, New Orleans, San Francisco, and Carson City, Nevada.

The $20 Liberty was a symbol of wealth around the world and was in consistent demand around the world as a unit of exchange. Because of its substantial value, few of these coins remain in Choice or Gem Uncirculated states of preservation. For the purposes of an eight-piece type set, let me focus on the coins struck from 1990 to 1907. Only 4,951 coins have been graded MS-65 by NGC and PCGS and only 1,991 have been graded. Only 270 have been graded MS-66.

So, it's with little hyperbole that I stress this coin will be the hardest to obtain in either Choice or Gem Uncirculated condition. The most common surviving coins from this series post-1900 are the 1904 Philadelphia. Stay away from these 1904 common dates in Choice MS-65 condition, and pay the premium for a 1900, 1901, 1902, 1903, 1906, or 1907. Paying an extra 20%-30% in this case should pay off nicely as gold takes off and sets the rare coin market on fire. When locating an MS-66, a 1904 is just fine.

The projected price of these gold coins at the following gold prices

	$340	$450	$550	$675	$750	$1,000
MS-65	$3,000	$5,000	$7,500	$10,000	$14,500	$18,500
MS-66	$6,500	$11,750	$15,750	$21,500	$26,500	$43,500

Coin #8: $20 Saint-Gaudens (1907-1933), "Double Eagle"

The Saint-Gaudens $20 Gold Coin is the most famous gold coin in history. As I write this book the 1933 example of this magnificent coin holds the world's record high price at auction selling for $7.5 million!

After FDR's executive order making private gold ownership illegal, all of the 1933 $20 U.S. gold coins, which were still supposed to be at the mint (as none were released), were believed to have been melted by the mint, gold yielded, and transferred to Fort Knox.

However, it has been speculated and rumored for the past six decades that one or more examples were smuggled out of the U.S. Mint before they were melted. Some numismatic historians believe this coin was not smuggled but was in fact given as a gift by mint officials to King Farouk, Egypt's last monarch. Farouk is one of the last century's most famous rare coin collectors.

This coin re-emerged in 1996 and came into the possession of Stephen Fenton, who is a well-known and respected rare coin dealer based in London, England.

Fenton smuggled the coin into the United States and was apprehended with the coin after attempting to sell it to undercover Secret Service agents in New York. Since the origin and the legality of this 1933 Double Eagle was clearly clouded and in question, the U.S. government agreed to an out-of-court settlement with Fenton last year, the terms of which mandated the sale of the coin at auction and proceeds to be split. Fenton also agreed to pay an additional $20 cash back to the U.S. government in order to balance the books.

An anonymous bidder paid the sale price of $6.6 million for the 1933 Double Eagle, a 15% commission to Sotheby's and the coin's $20 face value.

This sale was an important turning point for rare coin collectors and investors. It showed that serious money is making its way from Wall Street into hard assets and collectibles.

I do *not* recommend buying this 1933 Saint Gaudens $20 or any others that might resurface (rumors persist that two to four additional coins exist). I do recommend including a pre-1933 Gem Uncirculated MS-66 or even a Gem MS-67 example. There have been many hoards of these coins sold into the market. These $20 gold coins were very popular in Europe and when FDR signed his executive order, many of these coins found their way to European banks. They were the most common balance of payment accepted by European banks for U.S. debt.

I personally have bought and sold several thousand of these coins, and while you can coin Gem quality MS-66 coins common they are available. NGC and PCG have graded 20,372 coins. "Saints" were struck with a motto in 1907, and without a motto in 1908. The most common dates are 1908, 1924, and 1927. They were struck in Philadelphia, Denver, and San Francisco. The design is also currently used for U.S. bullion coins issued by the U.S. government from 1988. They are NOT rare. See the chapter on bullion coins.

The following table shows my price projections for Gem Uncirculated MS-66 and MS-67 condition $20.00 Saint-Gaudens struck from 1908 to 1932 based on the combination of higher gold prices and growing number of collectors and investors. Please note these projections are for coins that are "common" but not dated 1908, 1927, or 1928. Dates I like are: 1911-D, 1914-S, 1915-S, 1923-D, 1925, 1926 and 1928, which trade at a slight premium over 1908, 1924, and 1927 examples. I also think paying 40% extra premium for a 1907 or 1910-D makes good long-term investing sense.

The projected price of these gold coins at the following gold prices

	$340	$450	$550	$675	$750	$1,000
MS-66	$2,200	$3,500	$6,500	$9,000	$12,500	$18,500
MS-67	$7,850	$10,250	$14,000	$18,500	$23,500	$31,500

A final word for these wonderful Saint-Gaudens $20 Gold Coins: In 1907 a small number of these coins were struck in high relief. These coins are magnificent. If you start buying gold coins, you'll want one of these. Each coin was struck several times so that Miss Liberty literally pops off the coin, much like the coin designs of ancient Rome, Egypt, and Greece. These coins trade for as much as $27,500 in Choice Uncirculated and $45,000 in Gem MS-66 condition. They come with a "flat rim" and "wire rim." PCGS and NGC have graded just 146 coins of these two types combined.

The projected price of these gold coins at the following gold prices

	$340	$450	$550	$675	$750	$1,000
MS-65	$25,500	$33,000	$45,000	$52,000	$61,500	$80,500
MS-66	$45,000	$60,250	$85,000	$100,000	$125,500	$175,000

Proof Coins

No doubt if you follow my recommendation and buy an eight-piece 20th Century U.S. Gold Type Set in Gem condition you'll run across the term proof. A proof coin is made from specially selected coin blanks that have been highly polished and dies that are also highly polished. The coins are hand fed in a slow-moving press at the various U.S. Mints. They are struck multiple times to make sure the coins details are superior to those that are made for circulation. The Liberty Gold Coins in proof condition have high mirror surfaces. The Indian Gold Coins were produced with matte surfaces. The twentieth century gold coins I've recommended in this eight-piece type set are VERY rare in Gem Proof condition. I don't recommend them as an investment unless you are investing $75,000 or more in the gold rare coin market. They have tremendous investment potential, but should only be sought once you've completed the eight-piece twentieth Century Type Gold Set that I've recommended in this chapter.

Chapter 11
Modern Commemorative $5.00 Gold Coins and Intelligent Gold Play

One of the best physical gold investments on the market is a special group of commemorative U.S. $5 gold coins struck from 1986 through 2002. All of these coins were struck at the West Point Mint and exhibit a very prominent "W" mint mark.

While there were many commemorative issues including silver dollars, half dollars, and even $10 gold coins struck by the United States since 1984, it is this group of $5 gold commemorative coins that I believe has the most profit potential. For example, the coin issued in this $5 commemorative series features a beautiful 1986 $5.00 Statue of Liberty Coin which marked the 100-year anniversary of France's gift of the statue to America.

The 1986 Statue of Liberty Coin has the second highest mintage of the series but is *still* very rare with a mintage of only 500,000 in proof and Mint State condition combined. The pre-issue price was $170 and the regular issue price was $175 for the Proof and $160 to $165 for the uncirculated coin. Initial demand was so great for this coin — the first $5 gold coin produced in more than fifty years — that the price skyrocketed to more than $500 for the Mint State and $700 for the Proof!

After the frenzy and excitement at the birth of this new commemorative series faded, the price of these coins on the open market slowly fell. Today each of these coins can be purchased graded and certified by PCGS or NGC in MS-69 or Proof 69 condition for less than $200 a coin. "Raw" or ungraded coins can be bought for less than $150. If you buy any of these raw coins it is important to make sure you obtain the original packaging when the coins are delivered to you. Years from now you'll see a strong price on resale. But the bottom line is that NGC- or PCGS-graded coins MS-69 or PR-69 are recommended.

After the tremendous success it had selling the $5 Gold 1986 Statue of Liberty, the mint officials, in their wisdom, figured that if they could sell 500,000 Half Eagles why not raise the authorized mintage to 1,000,000? Why not raise the price on the next commemorative $5 produced, too? And that's exactly what they did.

The next coin in the series was a wonderful 1987-W Constitution $5; it had a pre-issue price for the Proof of $200 and the regular issue price of $225. The Uncirculated pieces were issued at $195 to $215; 214,225 Uncirculated and 651,659 Proofs were distributed that year.

Mint officials were almost correct in their thinking with a total of 865,884 pieces sold. The public figured it would buy these pieces and wait for the prices to climb just like the 1986 Statue of Liberty Coins. Unfortunately for them, the euphoria surrounding the first issue never carried through to the 1987 issues and the prices plummeted from the issue price. These $5 Constitutional Commemorative Coins currently sell for only 25% over melt. Coins graded and certified by NGC or PCGS in PR69 or MS-69 condition sell for about $195 each; I think they represent wonderful values.

The mintage of $5 Commemoratives declined to 344,378 in 1988 and 211,589 in 1989. No $5 Commemoratives were issued in 1990. The mint resumed striking coins in 1991 with the issue of the Mount Rushmore Commemorative. The public had clearly begun to lose interest in the program with only 143,950 $5 coins sold.

Two coins types were issued in 1992: the Columbus and the Olympic. The Olympic Coin was issued to help support the training of American athletes participating in the 1992 Olympic Games. Slightly more than 100,000 of each were sold.

The Madison $5 was issued in 1993. This was the first year that sales rose since 1988, but only by about 10%. 111,917 combined

Proof and Uncirculated coins were sold. In 1994 the sales dropped again to 90,688 for the World War II Commemorative. The 1994 issue commemorated The World Cup of Soccer. The mint expected worldwide demand for the coin but only 112,061 were sold.

The year 1995 brought an onslaught of $5 Commemoratives from the U.S. Mint. Four different coins were issued for the 1996

Atlanta Olympic Games and a Civil War Coin was also struck. The public at this point finally had enough overproduced and overpriced coins from the mint. The sales dipped to all-time lows for the Modern $5 Commemoratives. A total of 67,538 Civil War Coins were struck. The Olympic $5 Gold Coins were dated 1995 and 1996 and were produced at the West Point Mint.

The Olympic Coins issued in 1995 and 1996 along with mintage figures are:

Coin	Proofs	Uncirculated
1995 Torch Runner	57,442	14,675
1995 Stadium	43,124	10,579
1996 Cauldron	38,555	9,120
1996 Flag Bearer	32,886	9,174

With mintage for some of the Olympic coins declining to less than 10,000 the aftermarket price exceeded the issue for the first time since 1986! The sales remained low in 1996 with the issue of the Smithsonian $5 coin; 21,722 Proofs and 9,068 Uncirculated coins were sold. Two $5 coins were issued in 1997; F.D.R.: 29,474 Proofs and 11,991 Uncirculated coins were sold.

The F.D.R. Coins in both Proof and Uncirculated sell for above its issue price today. This brings us to the least popular coin at the time of issue and the most popular coin in the current market. 24,072 Proofs and 5,174 Uncirculated $5 coins were issued to commemorate the fiftieth anniversary of Jackie Robinson breaking the

color barrier in Major League Baseball. The Proof was issued at $195 pre-issue, $225 regular issue. The Uncirculated price was $180 pre-issue, $205 regular issue. These coins are now worth more than $1,000 graded MS69 for Uncirculated coins today!

The Jackie Robinson $5 Gold Commemorative coin, Uncirculated, is the key to the set. A mintage of only 5,174 ranks with some of the true gold rarities of all Federal issue gold coins. This is not a "rare coin of the near future," it is a rare coin today just five years after it was issued!

The poor sales of the Jackie Robinson Commemorative meant that no coins were struck in 1998. The series looked in genuine trouble. But in 1999 the mint struck a gorgeous new George Washington $5 coin that reinvigorated the series. Part of the new interest in these $5 commemoratives was caused by the skyrocketing price enjoyed by the Jackie Robinson Commemorative.

When the public saw the 1997 Jackie Robinson Uncirculated appreciate to several times the issue price, the mint figured it would cash in and a total of 64,204 George Washington Commemoratives were sold. Despite the brisk sales and frenzy, the Washington $5 gold's didn't skyrocket in price like the Jackie Robinsons. Only recently have the coins traded slightly above the issue price of $195/$225 Proof and $180/$205 Uncirculated.

No $5 coins were issued in the year 2002. This really made no sense to me. After all, why would the mint not issue a $5 Commemorative to celebrate the second millennium? It was a foolish decision.

In 2001 the Capitol Visitor's Center $5 Gold coins were issued. There were several purchase options. The regular price was $225 for Proofs and $205 for Uncirculated. Sales again dropped to very low levels; this apparently was due to the lack of interest in the design of the coin and the failure of the 1999 $5 George Washington to rise in value, so only 6,748 of the Uncirculated Capital Visitor's coins sold.

This coin is already selling for more than $900 and we predict it will trade for more than $1,500 by the end of the 2005 in MS-69 condition. If gold runs up to $1,000 an ounce as I suspect it will these coins could easily trade hands for $2,500.

The 2002 $5 coins were issued to commemorate the Salt Lake City Winter Olympic Games. The mintage of this most recently struck $5 gold commemorative was only 5,727 in Mint State and 8,882 in Proof condition. I believe that this extremely low mintage issue makes these coins a MUST buy at the current price levels of just $350 in MS-69 condition and $325 in PR69 condition. At $1,000 gold, these coins should trade at between $1,500 and $2,000.

What to Buy, and a Few Words About Grading

I recommend collecting and investing in Modern Commemoratives in the grade of PCGS or NGC MS-69/70 or Proof-69/70. Enough of these coins exist that acquiring them is possible. I also recommend buying an entire set as opposed to just the few really rare coins in the series. Complete sets in a hot gold market will be worth a 10% to 25% premium.

PCGS and NGC both have created "Set Registry Programs." You can register your coins and compete against other collectors for a set ranking with these programs. The Registry Set Program is an ingenious invention as one of the most important factors of supply and demand and price is involved — ego!

Bottom line: Everyone wants the best!

These $5 Modern Commemorative Coin Sets have tremendous potential in that they are legitimately rare coins that embrace wonderful events and people from U.S. history; and that makes them extremely collectable. But what I like most about this series is its gold content and how little more than the actual melt of the coins you have to pay to obtain them. Buying these coins is like buying beachfront property in Palm Beach, Florida for 1971 prices.

A $15,000 investment could easily return $45,000 or $60,000 as the price of gold crosses the $1,000 barrier.

Author's note: As I was writing this chapter something occurred to me. What if the prices of these wonderful modern Commemorative $5 Gold Coins move up sharply between my writing and the release of this book? The only solution I could come up with was to first warn my readers that prices are subject to both up and down moves, and to take a small position for myself in these coins, so I would have some on hand for those wanting to acquire them. As with any rare coin I sell, I work on a small 10% profit. I have a small number of these coins available and you can reach me at www.FinestKnown.com or 561-750-1716. I always try to speak to every client directly. Since this area is a passion for me, I enjoy talking to new and experienced gold and rare coin investors.

Chapter 12
Investing in Gold Mutual Funds

I prefer to invest in gold directly, since rare gold coins are my favorite gold investment. I strongly encourage you to always have some physical gold in your portfolio; gold coins are probably the best way to do this. Gold mutual funds could be a suitable alternative for some investors such as IRA investors or investors on a budget. This chapter is not going to be a complete guide to mutual fund investing but we will try to give you some sound advice that you can use to help you select a gold mutual fund that meets your needs.

A mutual fund is a fund operated by an investment company that raises money from shareholders and invests in actual gold, stocks, bonds, options, or money market securities and investments that are authorized by the fund charter. The fund is actively managed by a professional money manager. The investor has a share of the professionally-managed portfolio. Mutual funds issue and redeem shares on a continual basis; they can be purchased directly through the mutual fund company or through a broker. Most funds are not available on an exchange; although Exchange Traded Funds (ETFs) are becoming more prevalent.

Timing your buy and sell decisions is not as important for mutual funds, especially if the mutual fund manager is smart, experienced, and has a good track record. You do not want to second-guess a good money manager by trading in and out.

Many investors have a significant amount of their investable funds in retirement accounts. Because retirement account investors can't invest directly into gold due to investment regulations, gold mutual funds are an alternative. The best alternative is the gold exchange-traded trust that we will discuss later in this chapter.

How Does a Person Make Money in Mutual Funds?

Mutual funds work differently than owning gold or a stock. Investors in mutual funds can make money in three possible ways:

1. **Price appreciation:** An investor buys shares in a fund. The portfolio could consist of actual gold, gold mining stocks, diversified mining stocks, and cash. The share price would be the value of the portfolio minus management and operating expenses divided by the outstanding shares. In this example, we could say that at the beginning of the year the portfolio value minus expenses was $100 million divided by its ten million shares, giving a value of $10 a share. This $10 is considered the net asset value (NAV). The NAV is quoted in most newspapers. If the price of gold continues to rise the value of the shares will increase to $11 by the end of the year. The appreciation of the fund would be 10%.

2. **Capital gains:** Remember that your mutual fund is actively managed. Let's say that the portfolio manager sold some stocks in the portfolio, some at a loss and some for a gain, for a net capital gain of 50 cents per share. This would give you a capital gain of 5%.

3. **Dividends:** Some of the stocks and money market securities may throw off some income. For example, let's say the dividend is 17 cents. I have broken down the total return below.

   Appreciation from $10 to $11 =10%
   Capital gain distribution of 50 cents = 5%
   Dividend and income of 17 cents = 1.7%

   Total return is 16.7%

A prospectus will break down the total return for you. Some online resources will also detail the total return.

SEC regulations require that the dividends and accumulated capital gains will be "distributed" to shareholders periodically. Shareholders have a choice of taking the distributions in cash or in the form of additional shares in the fund. Check with your fund to learn about the distribution choices your fund offers. The gains have been accruing in the fund along the way, but once the distributions are made the fund will have a lower NAV similar to a stock that goes ex-dividend. In this example the NAV would drop by 6.7% (capital gain and dividend distribution). A person who decides to take a cash distribution will have a lower NAV; a person who reinvests will have more shares and a lower NAV. It is the portfolio manager's goal to increase the NAV. Mutual funds work ideally in retirement accounts. If you are investing in mutual funds in a taxable account, the capital gains reporting can get a little tricky so make sure you consult your tax advisor or financial planner.

Benefits of Gold Mutual Funds

Mutual funds are a very good vehicle for the small investor, IRAs, and other retirement accounts. It would be very difficult for a small investor to duplicate the diversification and professional money management of a mutual fund. I have listed several benefits of mutual funds below:

1. **Diversification:** Mutual funds give the investor the ability to own a share of a much larger portfolio that is diversified. This could be a plus and a minus. The main idea behind diversification is to reduce your risk by not having all your eggs in one basket. There are times where money managers diversify too much and the benefit of gold is diversified away. They may invest in government treasuries, service providers to gold mining companies, and companies that mine gold and other precious metals like silver and platinum.

2. **Professional Money Management:** To be a truly good stock picker a person needs education, intelligence, experience, training, and talent. He must understand business, economics, accounting, finance, marketing, leadership, management

and the dynamics of the market. To be a good gold stock picker it helps to have experience and knowledge of the gold industry; it also helps to have gold industry contacts and relationships.

3. Most mutual funds have **low investment minima**, a few as low as $50 for IRA accounts. Normally this can be important for young investors or investors on a budget. In our tables at the end of the chapter we have listed the investment minima and additional investment minimums. Most have low minima requirements for IRAs.

4. **Services:** Many mutual fund companies provide shareholder services. Services include quarterly statements, dividend and reinvestment plans, semi-annual updates from the fund manager, customer service support via 800 numbers, and automatic investing plans. Make sure you are familiar with all the services your mutual fund offers by asking your broker or calling the mutual fund company.

There are a few drawbacks to mutual funds. Funds do not always perform like gold because they have securities and other non-gold investments. We also learned that there are costs and fees involved with gold funds; you have to be careful to understand all your costs as they can be a drag on performance.

One concern that investors worry about lately is the consolidation of the mutual fund industry and fund manager changes. You may buy a fund because of the performance of the money manager; if that manager leaves then investor is then left to decide to sell, or to wait and see how the new manager performs. There has been a lot of consolidation among mutual fund companies so the company, fees, services, and portfolio manager could change in the future.

How to Select a Mutual Fund

One of the advantages of investing in this gold bull market versus the last one is that there are more mutual funds available. But this is also one of the *disadvantages* of this bull market because there are a lot more mutual funds from which to choose, which makes it more difficult to make a decision. Fortunately there are online services that can help you narrow your choices so that you can select a fund that meets your needs. Here are some important criteria to consider:

1. **Performance:** This is obviously the most important factor to consider. Many services will give you a ten-, five-, or three-year track record. The ten-year track record is the most important track record to review as it will include good and bad years and at least two business cycles (most business cycles last three to five years). You also want to look at bad years such as 1996 to 1998. How did the managers do in a bad period compared to the actual price of gold and other fund managers? Most money managers can make money when gold is moving up, but the really good managers distinguish themselves in bad gold markets by protecting the portfolio. There are many defensive measures a fund manager can take to protect the portfolio: move to cash or treasuries, invest in gold stocks that are diversified, and hedge with options or futures (not all funds allow their managers to hedge).

Try to make sure that the funds you are interested in have at least a five-year track record. That way you can judge how they perform in good and bad years.

When comparing performance of these funds, you should ignore ratings that compare gold funds to the S&P 500 or some other broad index. Gold funds are a specialty item often correlated to the stock market (which is what you want). Compare them instead to other gold funds.

2. **Management:** Normally if the fund has good long-term performance, it will have a good manager. The qualities of a good gold money manager include experience in the gold industry, intelligence, education, training, investment experience, contacts in the industry, and knowledge of the markets. Many mutual fund companies consider an MBA from a top-tier university and a CFA (Chartered Financial Analyst) designation (which is a minimum education requirement) for their

money managers. This is a very good idea because this background gives them a solid foundation in evaluating businesses, the economy, and corporate valuations. It's also important that the gold money manager has either worked for a gold mining company or has an undergraduate degree in geology or engineering. Morningstar Mutual Fund Reports will have some basic background information on a portfolio manager, such as education, designations, and tenure. The prospectus should have more background information on the mutual fund manager.

3. **Diversification:** With most mutual funds, diversification is a good thing since it allows you to participate in different sectors in the economy as well as reduce risk. For gold mutual funds too much diversification can reduce the non-related aspect of gold, where the fund will act more like a financial asset and not like gold. There are online tools that can help you determine the composition of the fund. Make sure that there are not too many stocks in the mutual fund and that the companies in which the mutual fund invests deal directly with gold.

Also, make sure that there are not a lot of diversified mining companies or suppliers to mining companies in the mutual fund. I have provided a list of mutual fund companies at the end of this chapter and some will have precious metals as part of their names. The precious metal companies may be funds that you want to avoid. There are some merits of a diversified precious metals fund as the flexibility could work in the long run, but to take advantage of our gold forecast at $1,000 an ounce you will want a fund that mimics gold as much as possible.

Also make sure that the turnover (number of times a year the portfolio changes) is not high and there are not high levels of cash. It makes sense for the money manager to change the portfolio to be more defensive when gold is in a bear market, but not in this environment.

4. **Fees: No-loads/loads.** Fees can be broken down into two types: management fees and loads (commissions). All funds will have management fees but not all funds will have a load.

Management fees can be less than .5% or more than 2% per year. The fund calculates its returns and fund value net of fees; you are not charged fees directly. A high fee structure could certainly be a drag on performance. There are very few fund managers whose performance is good enough to overcome high fees.

There are basically three ways to buy funds in terms of loads:

1. **No load:** Many financial publications advise no-load funds, since they allow you to buy the fund at NAV (Net Asset Value) without commissions. If you're willing to do your own research and you have the experience and knowledge to select a mutual fund, then I don't have to tell you that a no-load is probably your best choice. If you go directly to the fund, its staff can help you learn more about the funds but it will probably not be objective about its own funds. Some discount brokerage firms do have staff with the expertise to help you select a fund that may meet your needs. If you get some help from a discounter, make sure you ask someone with the appropriate experience and background. There is plenty of online help to assist you in learning about mutual funds and how to select a fund that meets your needs.

2. **Load:** A load fund is sold at the NAV plus commission but is redeemed at the NAV. Let's say there is a 5% load and the NAV is $10; you would add 5% to the NAV so you would pay $10.50. Normally load funds are sold by brokers. Most brokers at the big firms do not offer no-load funds. If you have a broker or financial adviser that you trust and have a good relationship with, he can help you select a fund that would be appropriate for you. Make sure you hang on to the fund for a long period of time so that you can spread the cost of the load over many years.

3. **Back-end loads:** To compete with load funds, brokers introduced back-end load funds. You buy the funds at NAV and they have a sliding scale charge to sell. They normally start at 5% for the first year and slide to no charge to sell if you hold for more than five years. The one caveat with these

funds is their management fees are normally much higher than no-load or load funds.

A subset of the back-end loads are funds that charge a redemption fee; if the fund is sold early these fees are normally a lot less expensive. A typical redemption fee would be 2% if the investor sells before sixty days. After sixty days there is no redemption charge typically.

Mutual Fund Resources

There are excellent resources and online tools to help you find and analyze mutual funds. The most well-known resource is Morningstar. I remember when Morningstar started in the late 1980s. It's come a long way with great improvements in the resources that it has for mutual fund investors. Its Web site has some free services as well as some subscription services if you decide to become a heavy mutual fund investor. Their Web site is www.morningstar.com.

Yahoo has an excellent mutual fund service in its Yahoo Finance Section, which can be found at http://finance.yahoo.com. MSN money also has a useful mutual fund section. Many online brokers and traditional brokers have online mutual fund screening tools and information. Most brokers and discounters have free literature to help investors learn about mutual funds. Ask your broker what literature is available through his firm.

Don't forget to read the prospectus. Regulators have forced mutual fund companies to make their prospectuses investor-friendly. There is a wealth of information out there which will help you learn a lot about a fund, its historical performance, objectives, fees, background information of the portfolio manager and investment company, and risks.

Mutual Fund List

I have put together a list of mutual funds that that can help you select a fund that meets your needs. There are more funds available but some were too small, or performance was not competitive, or they were closed to new investors. You will notice that many of the big-name money managers: Fidelity, Vanguard, Franklin, and Oppenheimer have a gold or precious metals fund.

The first list focuses on performance with the top three-year performers listed first. The last row in that list has the S&P 500 performance so you can compare how gold has performed against the S&P 500. Notice that gold outperformed the S&P 500 in the last five years and when the S&P 500 had a good year, gold did not and vice versa. This negative correlation will help your overall portfolio perform better with lower risk. The second list has the same mutual funds as the first list, but it is in alphabetical order and provides fee and initial investment minimum information.

The best performing fund is the First Eagle Gold Fund. It has the best performance for five and three years, and the best one-year performance during the worst year for gold in 1997. This disproves many financial experts' advice to avoid load funds. If the manager is good enough, he can sometimes more than cover the fund's fees and commissions.

I reviewed the Gold Mutual Funds available in 1980, and there were fewer funds available. Today's investors have a lot more choices and excellent tools and resources to help find and evaluate funds.

Mutual Fund List

Fund Name	3-year (%)	5-year (%)	10-year (%)	Best Year (%/2002)	Worst Year (%/year)
First Eagle Gold	37.82	18.24	N/A	107	-29.8 1997
Gabelli Gold	34.02	13.37	N/A	87.2	-51.9 1997
USAA Precious Metals & Minerals	33.4	17.99	2.17	67.6	-38.2 1997
Tocqueville Gold	32.9	N/A	N/A	83.3	-10.7 2000
Evergreen Precious Metals	30.26	14.68	N/A	72.4	-13.4 2000
American Century Global Gold Inv.	28.80	7.35	-1.24	73	-41.5 1997
Vanguard Precious Metals	25.87	16.68	1.75	33.4	-38.9 1997
Van Eck International Investors	24.94	8.86	-2.23	91.3	-36 1997
ING Precious Metals	24.85	8.52	.02	66.7	-43 1997
Fidelity Select Gold	23.64	13.97	2.59	64.3	-39.4 1997
AXP Precious Metals	21.64	10.3	2.14	60.8	-49.3 1997

Fund Name	3-year (%)	5-year (%)	10-year (%)	Best Year (%/2002)	Worst Year (%/year)
US Global Investors Gold Shares	21.56	-2.25	-13.40	81.4	-57.4 1997
Invesco Gold & Precious Metals	19.95	3.92	-4.38	59.7	-55.5 1997
Franklin Gold & Precious Metals	18.75	13.06	1.28	37.4	-35.7 1997
Rydex Precious Metals	16.75	5.3	N/A	48.2	-37.6 1997
Midas	15.14	-6.68	-5.56	61.1	-59 1997
Oppenheimer Gold & Special Minerals	N/A	N/A	N/A	42.3	N/A
S&P 500	**-10.30**	**-1.07**	**9.93**	**33.7 1997**	**-22.1 2002**

Fund Name	Minimum Initial Investment ($)	Minimum Additional Investment ($)	Load/ Redemption (%)	Fees (%)	Assets (mil. $)
American Century Global Gold Inv.	2,500 IRA	50	2 Rdmptn	.69	384
AXP Precious Metals	2,000 IRA 50	100	5.75	1.78	68
Evergreen Precious Metals	1,000 IRA 250	0	5.75	1.61	171
Fidelity Select Gold	2,500 IRA 250	500	3	1.24	595
First Eagle Gold	1,000 IRA 1000	100	5	1.66	203
Franklin Gold & Precious Metals	1,000 IRA 50	250	5.75	1.13	381
Gabelli Gold	1,000 IRA 1000	0	2 Rdmptn	1.67	178
ING Precious Metals	1,000 IRA 250	50	5.75	1.73	79
Invesco Gold & Precious Metals	10,000 IRA 1000	500	0	2.34	104

Fund Name	Minimum Initial Investment ($)	Minimum Additional Investment ($)	Load/ Redemption (%)	Fees (%)	Assets (mil. $)
Midas	1000 IRA 1000	100	0	2.58	44
Oppenheimer Gold & Special Minerals	1,000 IRA 500	50	5.75	1.45	200
Rydex Precious Metals	25,000 IRA 0	25,000	0	1.39	92
Tocqueville Gold	1,000 IRA 250	100	1.5 Rdmptn	1.68	223
USAA Precious Metals & Minerals	3,000 IRA 850	50	0	1.56	1.56
US Global Investors Gold Shares	5,000 IRA 0	50	0	3.57	44
Van Eck International Investors	1,000 IRA 0	100	5.75	1.96	220
Vanguard Precious Metals	3,000 IRA 1000	100	0	.6	487

Closed-End Fund

Another way to invest in gold is with closed-end funds. These funds have a fixed number of shares and sell on exchanges. They do not issue and redeem new shares every day like a mutual fund;

although they may make secondary offerings if demand is high they tend to specialize in a sector, country, or asset. Close-end funds trade at a discount or a premium to its NAV.

There is a gold closed-end fund called the Central Fund of Canada (**AMEX: CEF**) that invests exclusively in gold and silver bullion. The fund's objective is to hold at least 90% of its assets in gold and silver physical bullion. At the time of this writing the fund held 297,000 ounces of gold and almost fifteen million ounces of silver. But one problem is that the fund currently trades at an approximate 15% premium to the NAV, and that premium fluctuates.

As you can see below the fund does follow the price of gold fairly closely. The risk for the investor in CEF is not only that the price of gold could move adversely, but also that the premium above NAV could contract, making losses get magnified.

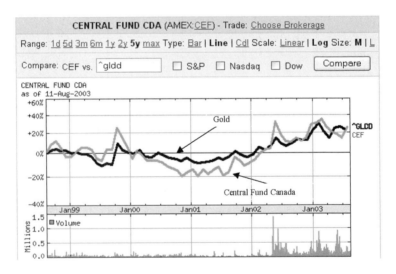

Figure 12.1: Central Fund Canada Price Performance Versus Gold

The premium/discount of CEF's share price to NAV tends to expand and contract along with rallies and declines in the price of gold. Some savvy gold traders have learned to use the level of this premium as a contrarian sentiment indicator for changes in gold prices.

Equity Gold Trust Fund (EGTF)

There is an exiting new gold investment that will be available to investors. The Equity Gold Trust Fund (EGTF) will invest in actual gold bullion; this investment will be the next best alternative to owning gold. EGTF will be very different from the traditional gold mutual fund. It will not be diversified, it will not invest in gold mining companies, and it will not be professionally managed. The trust would own gold bullion. Its shares are expected to be priced at 1/10 of an ounce of gold. At the time of this writing, that would be approximately $36.50.

If you bought 100 shares it would cost you $3,650 plus a brokerage commission, hopefully with discount broker commissions for your sake. It is planned that the actual gold will be deposited in vaults of the Hong Kong Shanghai Banking Corporation in London. The shares are expected to trade in London and Tokyo stock exchanges and potentially in Toronto and Johannesburg. In the U.S. they will trade on the New York Stock Exchange under the symbol GLD. The management fee is expected to be a very low .12%.

The advantage to the investor is that there are no transportation, warehousing, or security costs for buying and storing gold. The fund takes care of that for you for a very modest fee. You also do not have the typical markup that must be paid to a dealer for buying bullion.

At the time of this writing the EGTF shares are waiting for the Securities and Exchange Commissions' approval. The World Gold Council expects this product expected to be available in the second half of 2004.

As I mentioned, institutions and retirement accounts held by individuals are barred from owning gold directly, and they control trillions of dollars of investment funds. By allowing gold to be owned in the form of a stock, it will be eligible for these accounts. I believe that the demand for gold will explode with this event alone.

If you're going to invest in gold funds the EGTF is probably the best way to invest.

Chapter 13
Investing in Gold Stocks

I have had the pleasure of meeting some of the greatest stock pickers and stock market analysts. They have skill, talent, intelligence, education, experience, and a passion for investing. This chapter will not make you a great stock picker, but it can provide some guidance if you do want to develop your own portfolio of gold stocks.

I will begin with general comments, criteria, and strategies that you may want to consider in selecting your gold stocks. Some of the criteria you should consider when selecting your gold stocks include management, whether the company is pure (only gold producing) or diversified (producing various precious metals), hedged or non-hedged, leveraged or non-leveraged. There are different types of categories for stock selection (from an investment point of view). For example you can choose from companies with competitive growth rates, asset plays, gold stock leaders, and leveraged companies.

I used a database of more than eighty domestic and international gold stocks. The list of stocks and financial data presented here is available on many investment Web sites including brokerage firms' Web sites.

Price/Sales

The Price/Sales Ratio is used by many value investors and it answers the question, "How much are you paying for a dollar of sales?" Price is actually the market capitalization of the company, which is the current stock price multiplied by the company's shares outstanding. Sales are the amount of products, goods, and services that a company sells.

For instance, if you wanted to buy Microsoft you would multiply the current price of $26.47 by its shares outstanding, 10.8 billion shares. To own Microsoft you would have to pay $285.8 billion.

$26.47 (current price) * 10.8 billion = $285.8 billion

Microsoft's sales are $32.2 billion

So if you wanted to buy Microsoft it would cost you $285 billion for a company that made $32.2 billion of revenue in 2002.

Microsoft's Price/Sales Ratio would be 8.8
($285.8 Billion Price/$32.2 Billion Sales = 8.8)

In other words we are paying $8.80 for a dollar of sales. This is expensive but this is one of many measures we will look at. You never want to make a judgment based on only one measurement.

Let's look at another example to see the value of Price/Sales even though this example might be an extreme one. At the height of the technology bubble in 2000 Cisco was trading at around $80 a share. Cisco had 7.138 billion shares outstanding, so if you wanted to buy out Cisco it would cost you $80 * 7.137 = $570 billion dollars. Its sales in 1999 were slightly more than $12 billion. The question is would you pay $570 billion for a $12 billion company? A prudent investor would say **NO.** Those investors paid approximately $47.50 ($570/$12) for a dollar of sales.

This is a simple valuation that can be valuable in screening a stock. Professional investors like using Price/Sales because it is one of the most pure tools investors have to use. The price and market capitalization tell you how much are you paying for the company. There are many legal ways companies can manipulate earnings but there are very few ways you can manipulate sales legally. If a company is manipulating its sales it is probably committing fraud; and despite all of the attention that Enron and WorldCom got, outright fraud is not as common as people think.

Company Name	Market Cap. (mil. $)	Price to Sales
New Jersey Mining Company	5.35	1177.52
Coral Gold Corp.	6.43	1107.62
Apex Silver Mines Limited	552.01	678.29
Metallica Resources Inc.	39.87	421.59
Capital Gold Corporation	12.88	337.72

Figure 13.1: Most Expensive Gold Stocks per Price to Sales

Figure 13.1 shows the most expensive stocks from our gold stock database according to Price/Sales. You would pay $1,177.52 for a dollar of sales for New Jersey Mining Company.

Company Name	Market Cap. (mil. $)	Price to Sales
Centaur Mining & Exploration Ltd. (ADR)	1.1	0.01
North Lily Mining Company	0.03	0.03
Siskon Gold Corporation	0.13	0.07
Breakwater Resources Ltd.	28.49	0.22
Sterlite Gold Ltd.	19.88	0.49
Campbell Resources, Inc.	12.01	0.83

Figure 13.2: Cheapest Gold Stocks per Price to Sales

Figure 13.2 lists the cheapest stocks per price/sales. You could buy Centaur Mining's sales for 10 cents on the dollar. All the companies listed are very small companies.

Company Name	Market Cap. (mil. $)	Price to Sales
Anglo American plc (ADR)	23271.49	1.49
Newmont Mining Corporation	11525.06	4.15
Barrick Gold Corp.	9858.98	5.07
AngloGold Limited (ADR)	6981.3	3.67
Placer Dome Inc.	4893.7	3.37

Figure 13.3: Price/Sales for the Five Largest Market Capitalization Gold Corporations

Figure 13.3 lists the cheapest price/sales ratio for the five largest gold companies.

Price/Earnings (P/E)

Most investors are more interested in earnings and they should be. Earnings are essentially sales minus all expenses. Earnings eventually wind up in stockholder equity; this is the wealth of shareholders. The price-to-earnings ratio (P/E) answers the question, "How much am I paying for earnings?" Over time, the average P/E ratio for the stock market in general has been around 14 or 16. That means throughout history investors have paid around $15 dollars for $1 of earnings.

On the list, the average P/E for gold stocks is a high 45; for every dollar of earnings a gold company makes investors are willing to pay $45.

Company Name	Market Cap. (mil. $)	P/E
Anglo American plc (ADR)	23271.49	14.48
Newmont Mining Corporation	11525.06	40.96
Barrick Gold Corp.	9858.98	51.24
AngloGold Limited (ADR)	6981.30	20.47
Placer Dome Inc.	4893.70	27.97
Harmony Gold Mining Co.	2567.75	23.75
Goldcorp, Inc.	2145.02	33.16
Compania de Minas Buenaventura (ADR)	1793.03	12.91
Glamis Gold Ltd.	1489.34	99.92
Meridian Gold Inc.	1118.54	25.86
Lihir Gold Limited (ADR)	1056.09	24.99
Ashanti Goldfields Co. (ADR)	1029.96	17.52
IAMGOLD Corporation	737.65	100.78
Randgold Resources Ltd. (ADR)	490.22	10.42
Royal Gold, Inc.	422.14	31.52

**Figure 13.4: The Largest Market Capitalization Stocks and
Their P/Es in June, 2003**

Figure 13.4 does not include companies that had losses the previous year. You can't calculate a P/E if the company has losses. The cheapest stock is Royal Gold — investors would pay approximately $10 for one dollar of earnings. The most expensive stock on the list is IAMGOLD at $100 for one dollar of earnings.

Profitability

Companies with superior profitability are normally a reflection of superior management. Good management is able to sell, market, keep expenses under control and manage company resources. If it can do this, then it should see solid profitability. A company's ability to generate profits is extremely important for shareholders. There are many ways portfolio managers can judge a company's profitability; we will look at two.

The first measure we will consider is the profit margin, which is the relationship of gross profits to net sales. If the company sells something, what percentage of the sale does it get to keep?

Profit Margin = Gross Profits/Net Sales

Returns and allowances are subtracted from gross sales to calculate net sales. Cost of goods sold is subtracted from net sales to arrive at gross profit. Profit margins can be revealing when compared with the historical trend and with other gold companies in terms of the firm's operating efficiency, pricing policies and competitive pressures. A profit margin higher than industry and market averages is generally favorable.

Return on Equity (ROE) is the percentage return to a company's owners and shareholders. This measurement answers the question, "What is the return of a dollar invested in a particular company?"

ROE = Net Income /Stock Holders' Equity

A ROE higher than industry and market averages is favorable because it indicates the company generates higher-than-average returns on capital invested by shareholders. A very high ROE may also indicate that there is more debt than equity on the balance sheet. In our case since we are expecting much higher gold prices and are willing to take the risk, leverage could be an advantage. It is also good to look at a five-year historical comparison to determine consistency.

Company Name	ROE (TTM)	Market Cap. (mil. $)	Profit Margin (%)	Debt To Equity
Randgold Resources Ltd. (ADR)	86.91	490.22	41.2	0.28
Compania de Minas Buenaventura (ADR)	31.81	1793.03	81.46	0.10
AngloGold Limited (ADR)	23.32	6981.30	18.90	0.49
Goldcorp, Inc.	21.32	2145.02	34.67	0
Harmony Gold Mining Co.	16.42	2567.75	11.57	*NM*
Ashanti Goldfields Co. (ADR)	14.35	1029.96	10.03	0.69
Meridian Gold Inc.	11.08	1118.54	28.91	0
Anglo American plc (ADR)	10.75	23271.49	13.79	0.48
Lihir Gold Limited (ADR)	9.04	1056.09	18.76	0.10
Placer Dome Inc.	8.95	4893.70	11.64	0.46
Newmont Mining Corporation	5.82	11525.06	12.67	0.30
Barrick Gold Corp.	5.80	9858.98	9.91	0.30
Glamis Gold Ltd.	4.75	1489.34	14.93	0
IAMGOLD Corporation	2.70	737.65	6.65	0.04
Industry Average	6.08	450.03	14.55	0.25

NM = Not Meaningful

Figure 13.5: Gold Companies' Profitability

Figure 13.5 lists the gold companies with the best ROE and profit margins. Randgold Resources certainly has the best return on an invested dollar even with moderate leverage. Most investors will not invest in a company just because it has superior profitability, but that is one of the criteria that should be used.

Gold Reserves and the Cost of Gold

Probably the most important quality a gold company should have is high gold reserves. As the price of gold rises the companies with the highest gold reserves could become the most valuable. Reserves are labeled as *proven, probable, or possible.* Securities regulators and the accounting profession have rigorous rules that govern the labeling of reserves. To be proven, drilling and sampling of ore must be closely spaced. Since this is an expensive process, it is likely that mines will only prove a few years of production. Because of this, *proven reserves* are not a good indicator of the true life of the mine. *Probable reserves* are less rigorously defined.

The company's cost to produce gold is another important criteria to consider. As we mentioned previously, North America has a relatively low cost to produce gold. There are many factors that determine the cost of producing gold: labor, location, accessability, the depth of the deposits, the hardness of the rock, the amount of waste material that must be removed to mine the gold, and the cost of compliance with environmental regulations.

Company Name	Market Cap. (mil. $)	Cash Cost ($/oz)	Reserves (ounces) P & P
Anglo American plc (ADR)	23271.49	203	72.30 mm
Newmont Mining Corporation	11525.06	155	87.20 mm
Barrick Gold Corp.	9858.98	177	86.90 mm
Gold Fields Limited (ADR)	5867.43	183	79 mm
Placer Dome Inc.	4893.7	195	52.90 mm
Harmony Gold Mining Co	2567.75	225	49 mm
Kinross Gold Corporation	2190.31	220	13.20 mm
Goldcorp, Inc.	2145.02	99	5.50 mm
Compania de Minas Buenaventura (ADR)	1793.03	180	1.10 mm
Glamis Gold Ltd.	1489.34	170	5.70 mm
Meridian Gold Inc.	1118.54	87	4.20 mm
IAMGOLD Corporation	737.65	133	7.10 mm
Randgold Resources Ltd. (ADR)	490.22	74	11.50 mm
Hecla Mining Company	446.31	137	7.69 mm
Eldorado Gold Corporation	367.80	230	5.80 mm

P & P = Proven and Probable

Figure 13.6: Large Gold Companies Reserves and Cash Cost Per Ounce

Figure 13.6 is the most important table in this chapter. It shows the companies that have the highest reserves and lowest costs and which companies the market is valuing the most. The companies that have the lowest costs have the best chance of being the most profitable. The companies with the largest reserves have the potential of being the most valuable, especially if the price of gold meets my target of $1,000 an ounce.

There are several caveats on this list. First, some of the companies listed produce more than gold. Some also produce silver, platinum, copper, and other precious metals. Many of the companies are domiciled outside of the Unites States. International investing has currency, political, and regulatory risks that are normally higher than U.S. investing. Make sure to understand all the risks of international investing.

Earnings Growth

Most investors are very interested in earnings growth. It stands to reason that most investors want to accumulate wealth as quickly as possible, and earnings wealth is seen as helping investors do that. Figure 13.7 features gold companies with the best potential growth rates.

Company Name	Market Cap. (mil. $)	EPS Growth (5 year)
Barrick Gold Corp.	9858.98	108.20
Lihir Gold Limited (ADR)	1056.09	64.93
Richmont Mines Inc.	49.29	63.63
Compania de Minas Buenaventura (ADR)	1793.03	27.43
Placer Dome Inc.	4893.70	23.33
Royal Gold, Inc.	422.14	19.18
AngloGold Limited (ADR)	6981.30	17.80
Harmony Gold Mining Co.	2567.75	16.54
Anglo American plc (ADR)	23271.49	7.01

Figure 13.7: Gold Companies with the Best Potential Growth Rates

These growth rates are projected by analysts and they can certainly be inaccurate. There is no way anyone can be certain what will happen five years from now. The way to use this chart is to consider these the leading growing companies in the industry, but don't expect the growth rates to be accurate. Every quarter when earnings come out the stock price should reflect their growth rate.

If you are a growth investor, then these are the companies that you may want to consider.

Buying the Leaders

One strategy that money managers use to pick stocks is to stick with the industry leaders. Money managers will use management, stock price appreciation, profitability, growth, and the company's capital structure (the use of debt and stock issuance) as measures to discern leadership in an industry. In our case, the gold company with the lowest cost, highest reserves, best profitability, and best management and growth rates would be the ideal company. Normally a company with the least amount of debt would be considered a good attribute, but for our purposes leveraging an appreciating asset with debt could be profitable, so high debt could be a measurement we look at. Normally the strongest and best companies are also going to have the most expensive valuations in terms of their price/earnings and price/sales.

Some analysts believe that the large gold stocks will continue to do well and will attract large institutional investors (mutual funds, money managers, banks, insurance companies). Many institutional investors see the potential rise in the price of gold and will seek out the larger gold stock companies because they have more trading liquidity. They also believe it is likely there will be more consolidation in the industry as smaller rivals will have to merge to achieve the economies of scale of the larger companies. The institutions will do their homework to anticipate the next company that may be bought out.

Symb	Company Name	Market Cap. (mil. $)	P/E (TTM)	Profit Margin (%)	Price to Sales	ROE (TTM)	Debt To Equity	EPS Growth (5 Yr.)
ABX	Barrick Gold Corp.	9858.98	51.24	9.91	5.07	5.80	0.30	108.20
AU	AngloGold Limited (ADR)	6981.30	20.47	18.90	3.67	23.32	0.49	17.80
PDG	Placer Dome Inc.	4893.70	27.97	11.64	3.37	8.95	0.46	23.33
HMY	Harmony Gold Mining Co.	2567.75	23.750	11.57	2.57	16.42	*NM*	16.54
BVN	Compania de Minas Buenaventura (ADR)	1793.03	12.91	81.46	9.86	31.81	0.1	27.43
	Industry Average	450.03	45.31	14.55	6.19	6.08	0.25	-1.35

Figure 13.9: Large Capitalization Gold Stock Leaders

Figure 13.9 lists the companies with the best growth rates and profitability; most are reasonably priced compared to the industry average. Compared to the overall market these companies are expensive, but then again gold is not most companies' major asset.

You can also tell which ones are the market leaders by looking at a chart of the stock price. The markets are normally efficient and you can tell by the price chart which companies the market favors.

What follows are charts of the companies previously listed with the best price action. All three stocks are up approximately 50% from their lows. Placer Dome and Buenaventura have the best price charts as they have a "rising tops and bottoms" pattern which is bullish, whereas Anglogold has stopped moving up.

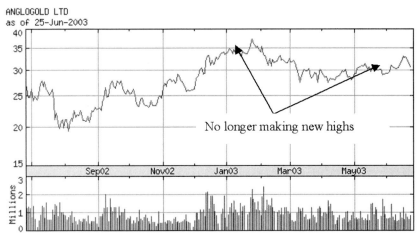

Figure 13.10: Price Chart of Anglogold Limited.

In Figure 13.10, Anglogold's chart we see the line stopped showing new highs.

Figure 13.11: Price Chart of Placer Dome

Placer Dome's chart (Figure 13.11) is showing higher highs and higher lows. Buenaventura's chart (Figure 13.12) is also showing higher highs and higher lows.

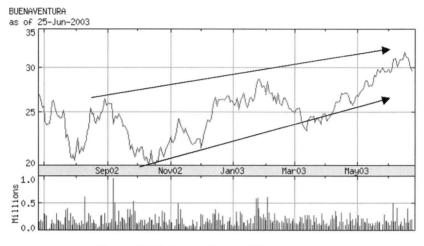

Figure 13.12: Price Chart of Buenaventura

Contrarian Investing

Being a contrarian investor means buying in the opposite way the industry leaders buy or buying stocks that nobody else is buying. Contrarian investors try to buy stocks that are undervalued and that nobody wants, hoping to sell them when they are fairly valued or overvalued. In other words they are trying to buy low and sell high.

Ashanti Goldfields has the lowest P/S ratio and Compania de Minas Buenaventura has the lowest P/E.

Company Name	Market Cap. (mil. $)	Price to Sales	P/E
Ashanti Goldfields Co. (ADR)	1029.96	1.73	17.52
Harmony Gold Mining Co.	2567.75	2.57	23.75
Kinross Gold Corporation	2190.31	3.30	*NM*
Hecla Mining Company	446.31	3.36	*NM*
Placer Dome Inc.	4893.70	3.37	27.97
AngloGold Limited (ADR)	6981.30	3.67	20.47
Randgold Resources Ltd. (ADR)	490.22	4.03	10.42
Newmont Mining Corporation	11525.06	4.15	40.96
Lihir Gold Limited (ADR)	1056.09	4.67	24.99
Barrick Gold Corp.	9858.98	5.07	51.24
IAMGOLD Corporation	737.65	5.27	100.78
Eldorado Gold Corporation	367.80	7.31	*NM*
Meridian Gold Inc.	1118.54	7.61	25.86
Agnico-Eagle Mines Ltd.	978.41	7.87	*NM*
Compania de Minas Buenaventura (ADR)	1793.03	9.86	12.91
Goldcorp, Inc.	2145.02	11.48	33.16
Glamis Gold Ltd.	1489.34	15.34	99.92
Royal Gold, Inc.	422.14	26.01	31.52
Industry Average	450.03	6.19	45.31

NM = Not Meaningful

Figure 13.13: Highest Market Capitalization Firms Ranked by P/S

Figure 13.13 shows the gold stocks that are the most undervalued per their price/sales and price/earnings ratios.

Gold Asset Plays

One strategy that is similar to contrarian investing is looking for asset plays. Most investors are looking for earnings growth and they forget about the underlying assets of the firm. This is especially true with gold stocks.

Gold stocks also have gold reserves — assets that are not always reflected in their share prices, and especially at our higher projected gold bullion prices; so we will look at companies that have lots of gold assets or potential gold assets. These are known as asset plays.

Company Name	Market Cap. (Mil. $)	Price of Gold $350 * Reserves Mil. Oz	Market Cap./ $ Reserves	Reserves Mil. Ozs P & P	Debt to Equity
Randgold Resources Ltd. (ADR)	490.22	4,025	0.12	11.50	0.28
Harmony Gold Mining Co.	2567.75	17,150	0.15	49	0.17
Eldorado Gold Corp.	367.80	2,030	0.18	5.80	0.06
Gold Fields Ltd. (ADR)	5867.43	27,650	0.21	79	0.18
IAMGOLD Corporation	737.65	2,485	0.30	7.10	0.04
Barrick Gold Corp.	9858.98	30,415	0.32	8.7	0.30
Kinross Gold Corp.	2190.31	4,620	0.47	13.20	0.04
Glamis Gold Ltd.	1489.34	1,995	0.75	5.70	0
Meridian Gold Inc.	1118.54	1,470	0.76	4.20	0
Goldcorp, Inc.	2145.02	1,925	1.11	5.50	0

Figure 13.14: Gold Stocks with Low Market Capitalization to Reserve Ratios

The underlined column header in the Figure 13.14 represents the market capitalization of the company divided by the potential dollar value of its reserves. The reserves are a combination of proven and probable (P&P). Let's look at Rangold Resources as an example. The ratio says that if you were buying the company, you would pay 12 cents on the dollar for the reserves. Remember, the reserves are estimates and it could take years to mine all the gold. As the price of gold increases, you can see that these companies could become very valuable. You would have to consider debt, since you would have the responsibility of paying the interest and at some point the principal. We can also see that most of these companies do not have a lot of debt.

Small Capitalization Gold Stocks

Some investors like to invest a portion of their investment dollar into aggressive, risky issues. Below is a list of companies that fit those wishes. There are several advantages of considering these risky shares:

1. They are often overlooked by Wall Street. You can make a lot of money by identifying opportunities before the crowd does.

2. They have small amounts of float (shares outstanding). It does not take a lot of trading volume to make these stocks move quickly. The downside is that they can also move down quickly.

3. If these companies can survive one of gold's worst gold bear markets, they can probably survive anything.

4. They can be potential acquisition candidates for larger gold companies.

5. Smaller gold companies are normally more entrepreneurial and are sometimes better at finding new discoveries.

If you are considering these smaller, riskier stocks (see Figure 13.15) make sure you buy several companies to diversify.

Symbol	Company Name	Market Cap. (Mil. $)	P/E (TTM)	Profit Margin (%)	Price to Sales	ROE (TTM)	Debt to Equity
MNG	Miramar Mining Corp.	140.08	116.00	1.12	1.88	0.49	0
RIC	Richmont Mines Inc.	49.29	6.88	16.45	1.11	30.13	0
GBGLF	Great Basin Gold Ltd.	47.34	*NM*	*NM*	*NM*	-36.40	0
GLDR	Gold Reserve Inc.	41.51	*NM*	*NM*	63.67	-4.36	0
VGZ	Vista Gold Corp.	40.52	*NM*	*NM*	*NM*	-45.78	0
METLF	Metallica Resources Inc.	39.87	*NM*	*NM*	421.59	-8	0.41
MKAU	MK Gold Company	29.92	*NM*	-21.40	7.88	-2.76	1.02
CAU	Canyon Resources Corp.	29.82	*NM*	-28.31	1.64	-15.53	0.06
BWLRF	Breakwater Resources Ltd.	28.49	*NM*	-9.98	0.22	-16.95	0.81
PMU	Pacific Rim Mining Corp.	28.27	*NM*	-15.81	1.74	-13.74	0.11
SLGLF	Silverado Gold Mines Ltd.	24.44	*NM*	*NM*	*NM*	-237.31	0.36
SGDTF	Sterlite Gold Ltd.	19.88	3.41	10.92	0.49	15.45	0.02

NM = Not Meaningful

Figure 13.15: Small Capitalization Gold Stocks

Conclusion

We have reviewed several criteria and strategies that one can use when selecting a gold stock. You can also review our buying and selling section to help you with the timing of your buy and sell decision. The stock ideas are just a starting place; it would certainly make sense to do your own due diligence on any stock before you invest.

Chapter 14
Investing in Canadian Junior Resource Stocks

Contributed/written by David and Eric Coffin

I am fortunate to have many contacts in the gold and investment community. I have asked David and Eric Coffin, experts in Canadian junior resource stocks (precious metals, base metals, diamonds), to contribute to this book; this chapter is written by them. They provide insight, vast knowledge, and experience in the areas of geology, resource exploration, Canadian stocks and resource investing. Investing in junior or resource stocks can be lucrative but it is very speculative.

Although this chapter is about investing in junior resource stocks, all of the concepts and tools can be applied to junior gold companies. Junior stocks are more speculative and require different analysis and skills to be a successful investor/speculator. It is best to follow a newsletter rather than try to invest or speculate on your own, especially if you're a novice. You can learn about their services and newsletter at www.hardrockanalyst.com.

Mining for Management

The greatest potential for percentage gains in any venture capital investment comes during the early financing stage of a company's history, when an idea is being worked into a plan of action. As befits the potential for high gains, this is also the investment point that is most likely to produce a failure. In the mine exploration business, even the best-laid plans will not work out from the grassroots level without an element of luck. Investors should look for companies that are acting in a manner that allows a discovery to happen.

This requires both a well-structured company and a well-structured exploration program with recognizable potential. The focus of this chapter is the financial and management attributes that help the company succeed. I will also address some of the important signs to look for when judging the early potential for exploration success.

The first section deals with the basics of choosing the right company at the right time based on the three Ms: money, management, and market timing. This section details how to review a company's current financial condition, money raising activities, and past share issuances. It continues with an overview of what to look for in a management group, what types of management background influence investors, and the general pros and cons of "big name" executives. The section concludes with some insight into the timing and manner in which news is released during the exploration process, what sort of news has the greatest influence on price, and when you should consider buying or selling on the release or imminent release of news.

The Three Ms:
Money, Management, and Market Timing

Money: The Primary Commodity

Exploration is an expensive business, and the rush by North American exploration companies to all parts of the globe has only increased the speed at which companies expend financial resources to explore for natural resources. Although classified by many outside observers as a "low-tech" business, modern exploration actually draws together experts from a wide range of scientific disciplines. The use of capital intensive geophysical and geochemical surveys, the expanded scope offered by remote sensing techniques, and the global nature of new projects at early stages of exploration have dramatically increased the cost of reconnaissance level work in the past couple of decades. Exploration efficiency has increased to the point at which small companies can take on very large property holdings and rapidly narrow down areas of interest for further study.

Before a company can get serious about project work, it has to raise money. One of the first questions you should ask a resource company is the level of its bank account and its *burn rate* — how quickly it's spending money. Unless you have convinced yourself that the company cannot fail in its exploration efforts (and you should *never* believe that), you should be sure that there are sufficient funds on hand to at least carry out the next program of work on the company's main properties, plus enough to cover overhead, administration, and investor relations until alternative financing can be arranged.

It is not uncommon for an IPO company to raise as little money as possible on the assumption that it will be able to finance at a higher price after its first phase of exploration. Ironically, the better the market is for resource companies, the greater likelihood that management will follow this minimalist approach to financing. The market treats exploration companies lacking money cruelly; be prepared to do some selling during the first exploration phase, or ride out the turbulence if the results are below the market's expectations.

Any company you are looking at should be able to give a fairly accurate estimate of the planned expenditures on each of its active properties and the time frame during which the money will be spent. This is information you will need in order to keep track of the information flow later (see "Market Timing" further on in this chapter). If a company cannot provide at least this level of detail on exploration expenditures, it should be avoided. A company is not properly organized if it has no exploration budgets that are contingent on either good or bad results.

Once you have found out how much money a company has you should find out exactly how it was made. To do this you can request a listing of the financings that have taken place over the last several years and the prices and terms of each financing. If you plan to make longer-term investments in a company, you should ensure that you are on the full mailing list as well. Many companies only mail out press releases to registered shareholders. Be sure that you are going to receive financial statements as well since they are often the best source of information on past financings. Companies listed on the Toronto Stock Exchange (TSX), for example, must list the prices and expiration dates of all outstanding options and warrants and the price and quantities of securities sold, in each quarterly statement. The best and quickest way to track most companies these days is the Internet. If you don't have www.sedar.com and www.edgar-online.com bookmarked, you should. SEDAR has a complete list of Canadian public companies with their filings included. All issuers are required to file virtually all their public documents with SEDAR, and other documents — such as technical reports, which are next to impossible to find anywhere else.

Unlike its U.S. counterpart, SEDAR is a free service and any investor can get up-to-date filings there. EDGAR is the U.S. version of this service although it's a little less organized than the Canadian version and there are sections that have a time delay if you are not a paying subscriber. While on EDGAR you should choose "text files only," which makes for quicker downloads, but means you lose all of the graphic content, which is often critical, especially with technical reports. Virtually any company you follow will have its own Web site, but some of the most useful documents, like recent prospectus filings, are not usually available there.

Essentially, you want to discover:

When did placements take place in the past, and at what prices?

When do or did these shares become tradable?

How many warrants and options are outstanding, and at what prices and expiration dates?

Were there or will there be large blocks of stock issued to acquire properties, and when may these shares be sold?

The ideal situation is one where the majority of the money raised came from sales of shares at a premium to the current market price and there has been no "bad news" to account for the drop in price. It isn't a common situation in a strong bull market, but it does occur in weaker markets, particularly if the company has not released significant news for a long time. While it is no guarantee of profits, there are definite advantages to being the "low person on the totem pole" in terms of share price.

It is important to know the terms of each placement since this determines the price at which these buyers can sell at a profit, and perhaps more important, when they can sell. Canada Private Placements, which are sold without a prospectus or offering document, have a hold period of one year unless the company has filed an Annual Information Form (AIF) in which case the hold period for most domestic buyers is four months. An AIF (or Form S2 in the U.S.) is one of the first things you should look for at the Web sites listed above. It tells you that the shorter hold period is in effect and is often the best-organized overview of the company and its affairs.

Shares sold by private placement manner go to "sophisticated investors," usually insiders or their close friends and business associates. Insiders (as defined by prevailing securities regulations) must report transactions in the stock and file an "Intent to Sell" statement if they plan to dispose of a significant portion of their holdings. Friends and associates do not have to report unless they hold more than 10% of the company's stock. You should view any large place who owns shares at a cheap price as a potential seller. The "standard" private placement these days is a "unit" which is comprised of one common share and a two-year warrant that allows the investor to purchase an additional share at the placement price in the first year and 15% above the placement price in the second year. Any shares acquired through the exercise of warrants are subject to the same hold period as the shares.

Management: Picking the "A" Team

Management is the most commonly cited reason for an independent recommendation of a junior resource stock when it is still in the reconnaissance stage. There are several reasons. The simplest explanation is that investors are more comfortable dealing with company management that has a strong track record when there are few other specifics to recommend the stock. This is an understandable viewpoint that we agree with, although we think that management is sometimes over-emphasized. Nonetheless, it's a fact of life for any venture company that the first two or three financings are the toughest to close, especially at a good price. Management is often the difference between an early financing that closes and one that does not. There are really two types of track records you should be looking for: exploration success and market success.

As a rule, management from an exploration background doesn't have experience dealing with the market; you should be sure that there is an investor relations program in place, run by people with a marketing background. Don't count on senior managers pounding the pavement to attract investors. If you are buying companies for technical management alone, you should also keep in mind that managers who have spent much of their careers with major companies are used to working with large budgets (in terms of both overhead and exploration work). Companies run by this type of management tend to have high burn rates and large overheads. There is nothing wrong with fair pay for superior management, but you have to keep an eye on the income statements — the money will disappear quickly. A past track record of discoveries is important, but it's the quality of properties it is working on now that will determine the future value of your investment. Don't lose sight of this.

Institutional investors in particular are willing to finance at higher prices if they trust management. This is obviously a plus, but it doesn't mean you should be paying high prices too. We have seen many companies in recent years which had $100-million plus market values, based on a set of grassroots properties and a group of senior managers from the majors. If you didn't get into these situations really early, it would be wise to wait for some exploration results before jumping on the bandwagon.

Here are a few points about management, and some management criteria you should consider:

- Management with strong "big company" background is particularly important to institutional investors and can help draw financing in the early stages.

- These financings are often needed since managers who are accustomed to having a large bureaucracy at their disposal tend to go through money at a rapid pace.

- Some extremely talented executives just won't work out when they move to the top job at a junior. A very different mind-set is needed to excel in an entrepreneurial, rather than a bureaucratic setting.

One setting where major company management is particularly helpful is foreign country experience. Investors have learned the hard way that local mining law, politics, and culture can have a major impact on project economics and a company's ability to operate. Management with local experience, often gained working for a major producer, can ensure things run as smoothly as possible and avoid major cultural or political gaffes.

Lightning doesn't always strike twice. The fact that a manager has been associated with past discoveries doesn't guarantee future ones. The reverse is also true. Most ore bodies are found by people who *haven't* found one before. Don't assume someone is a poor explorer if he does not have a couple of deposits to his credit already.

It is the market track record that is most important for investors to be aware of. A group that has had several market successes in the past will also easily find financing. If you can invest in one of these companies in its formative stages, you will usually see a good gain.

Although strong management will usually be able to finance more easily in good times and bad, the company will ultimately be valued on exploration success. The market premium of good management decreases over time.

Market Timing: Going with the Flow

Share prices sometimes seem to move in unpredictable and contrary ways. Changes in commodity prices, prevailing market sentiment, and third-party recommendations can heavily influence small-cap stocks. Exploration stocks which have no earnings to buoy their prices are particularly heavily influenced by rumor, speculation, and outside events. In the current market environment, investors are only going to follow a limited number of stories — the strength of the market for the commodity being explored for and the "buzz" about the region are very important in a hesitant market.

For individual stocks the greatest effect on prices over the medium term is the exploration results themselves. Investors continually re-evaluate their holdings based on information on hand and re-price stocks accordingly. It generally takes at least one phase of drilling for a company to develop a consistent market following, unless there are a significant number of impressive surface hard-rock results or a history of past results to go on. Until there are a couple of sets of drill results released the market will be trading on rumor, recommendations, and promotion. The management factor noted above also plays a part, but if you miss out on early "management-led" gains you can still use this to your advantage in other ways. You should make a habit of scanning news releases every now and then, looking for superior-looking results. This can be a time-consuming process which is why many investors leave this to the analysts. It can be rewarding, however, since you will sometimes come across a set of truly superior results from a project that had little or no impact on the share price due to bad timing of the news release, poorly written news release copy or simply a lack of market presence. While these factors often won't change by themselves, they can point to the potential for gains.

Check out the funding levels and working capital for the company. If the company has the funds on hand to keep delivering good results without going back to market, the odds of one of its future releases capturing attention are good. If the company proceeds to hire some professional investor relations group, see who they have worked for and check the companies out as well. If the Investor Relations Group succeeded in getting attention for other companies, its arrival might signal a buying opportunity. Conversely, if you are willing to go with your (or someone else's) instincts on the strength of the results, you may do well by accumulating and waiting for the market to come around for the stock. This is the essence of this kind of trading after all, reading between the lines and finding stocks that offer value *before* the market notices them.

The Area Play Strategy

Anyone who has been an active trader in the past few years is more than familiar with the concept of momentum stocks and momentum plays. These situations are attractive to investors for several reasons. These stocks have the safety of numbers and the liquidity that the market and media attention brings to them. They make it easy for the investor to justify his purchases because "everyone's doing it." And last but not least, they can generate good returns even for otherwise mediocre companies if the play is strong enough and the sector hot enough.

The resources sectors, be it precious metals, base metals, diamond, or oil and gas also have a form of the momentum play, known in the industry as the area play. Area plays develop when a company hits on a major discovery, one that dramatically boosts its share price. Just as companies reinvented themselves to be part of the "flavor of the month" tech sector, junior resource companies will rush in and stake claims near the discovery hoping some of the attention will rub off on them. If the discovery is exciting enough, a large group of companies in the area can suddenly be "in play" and there will be a series of profitable trading opportunities as exploration on the discovery project and the surrounding properties advances.

Of course, any investor experienced with momentum plays knows that they are definitely double-edged. It is almost inevitable that companies in a strong momentum play will become overvalued (absurdly overvalued in the case of many tech sectors in the Nasdaq bull market). Momentum plays can be very rewarding to those who trade them well, but disastrous to those who do not. It's critically important to understand that a strong momentum play will lift almost all participants, and that the "favored few" in any play will see some big price increases based on their similarity to the main drivers of the play, not their own merits — at least at first. Because of this, it's important to "trade smart" which, first and foremost, means TAKING PROFITS! If you are trading an area play, you are playing at the speculative end of the spectrum. You are counting on the market's enthusiasm for the play to do a lot of the heavy lifting, which by definition means you are expecting the stock to exceed reasonable levels of valuation. There's nothing wrong with this, but you need always keep the reality of the situation firmly in mind. If and when the market offers you a "free pass" in the form of a big gain before there are new exploration results or other data to back it up — TAKE IT. Trade your share cost down to zero or close to it; then you can follow the play in comfort rather than lying awake worrying about how the next set of discovery companies' drill results will stack up against the market's expectations.

Those of you who are not familiar with a classic area play can look to the diamond play in the Northwest Territories (NWT) for an example. At its height, there were more than 150 companies involved, tens of millions of acres staked and a cumulative market value in the billions. NWT has had satellite discoveries, one of which just went into production, and we expect there will be a couple more before it's done. This play is now eleven years old, and though it's relatively quiet, there have been a few periods of strong gains based on new discoveries, and those who have traded it well have seen a number of profit-making opportunities. It's an extreme example, but a trenchant one — area plays and the methods of trading them can be a very worthwhile addition to your arsenal of portfolio tools.

Here are some guidelines for choosing shares to buy in an area play:

1. Choose a portfolio of stocks. It's still too early to tell who will be successful. A selection of stocks is a much safer bet at this point. As exploration progresses, be prepared to shift these holdings around and probably narrow them down.

2. If possible, choose companies that are active on properties outside of the play as well. This gives the stock a fallback position. This is especially important if you are jumping in early. There are several "stillborn" plays each year. If you pick companies that have several "irons in the fire," you are much less likely to get hurt by a string of substandard results from the discovery company.

3. Look for experienced management. Many companies that jump on the bandwagon at this point have no mining experience and are just rolling the dice. This is the type of company that usually crashes hardest if things don't work out.

4. Look for some confirmation of the company's share price in the form of private placements. There will be a lot of companies trading at $2.50 who did their last financing at $0.25. Treat this as a danger signal if the company doesn't have concrete results to back up the current price. Whenever a company's share price is seeing these kinds of moves you want to see distribution at higher levels, otherwise there is a huge overhang of cheap stock that early investors will be looking to distribute at these high prices.

All things being equal, the bigger the properties controlled the better, especially if they are spread throughout the play. Companies with a lot of ground won't run out of a story as soon. A large land holding is usually the sign of a strong financing group.

Many companies will see their best price increases in the property acquisition and reconnaissance phases. Take profits if you are faced with a 300% to 500% profit and the drill hasn't even started turning yet.

Each area play has a few companies that investors and brokers really focus on, and they can provide some excellent gains. If this type of company has some moderate success during early surface work and the play is still hot, the market will almost always overvalue them. No company is worth $200-$300 million when it has nothing but a few surface results in. If you own this type of stock and the market is offering this type of return before the results are even in, take the money.

Unless you are bound and determined to just follow area plays, don't blind yourself to everything else in the market. Remember: Almost all great area plays are started by companies working "off the beaten track." If you focus too much on this play, you may miss the start of the next one!

Exploration and Information Flow

Investing in companies that explore for gold, diamonds, or other resources can be highly rewarding when done right, but picking winners early takes knowledge, skill and a little luck.

Exploration is the process of elimination, and this goes for companies as well as properties and mineral showings. A few points should always be kept in mind if you are trading the shares of companies that are this early in the exploration process on their projects. You should always practice portfolio investing, splitting your risk capital and buying shares in several companies at once. Be willing to take profits as things progress and don't be afraid to cut your losses when you need to.

The first phase of drilling usually has a HUGE impact on the value placed on a resource project, for good or ill. That's one reason it's so important to trade smart in the period leading up to drilling and the release of the first couple of sets of drill results. Ensuring a low holding cost through smart trading is one of the keys to long-term profits in the exploration game.

Exploration stocks display patterns of strong price movements around the release of significant information. The stronger the promotional ability of a company and the hotter the area where the property is located, the more pronounced these movements would be. Professional investors and traders who prefer to follow momentum and invest with very short time frames exacerbate this tendency. These investors will research a fairly large number of stocks and select a small number to monitor. They are looking for short-term trading situations that will provide both sufficient price change to make a profit and sufficient volume to make the situation worthwhile for a professional trader. The best opportunity in most cases will be the release by an exploration company of a large set of results that should contain enough information to allow the market to re-value the company's stock. Recommendations from outside analysts can have the same effect but they are not predicable events.

The important points regarding exploration finds and information flow:

- Information flow is critical since it is ultimately information that determines the price of the stock.

- Early phase reconnaissance results have less impact than later trench/drill results, and the effects of new results are usually stronger early in an exploration program.

- Major price moves are most likely when a company has reached a new exploration plateau with a project.

- Companies that release a series of results from an exploration program can hold investors' interest better than a company that releases all results in bulk and the end of each work program.

- Know how much news is coming and be wary about buying on a strong price increase if you know it will be several weeks or months before the next release of results.

Take a look at how a company has presented news in the past. Some companies are just better at putting results in the best possible light or explaining complex geological issues to investors. Some companies write news releases that are so boring or disorganized that anything but superior results will be totally ignored by the market.

Assessing Early Phase Prospects

A fundamental aspect of junior mining promotion over the years has been pitching "closeology," the proximity of a company's project to an existing deposit or mine. Unfortunately, the proximity usually relates to the map distance from the deposit rather than the conditions that represent a geological environment similar to those in which the type deposit developed. It is rare that more than a third of the companies in an area play are particularly close in a geological sense. Furthermore, the best gains are to be had by choosing companies that have sought out the right conditions away from the crowd, and are funded or can fund to carry exploration through to the next logical financing point.

An ore body has four basic dimensions. Three are length, width, and thickness that determine a physical volume eventually combined into a unit called tonnage. The fourth measure of the concentration of valuable constituent is called "grade." Tonnage is the capital component of a deposit and grade indicates operating viability; after allowing for minimum tonnage to carry the infrastructure costs of a given area, it is the minimum grade requirement over each of the three physical dimensions that determines the viability of a deposit. It is also important to know the size potential of the deposit being explored for. An understanding of potential related to other deposits in the area and the typical size range for the deposit type should be had before deciding to speculate on a company. If a company's market-cap is already approaching that of producers' mining typical examples of the target type, then the speculation is already in the market and you should move on to the next candidate.

Chapter 15
Hedging and Speculating with Futures

I realize that most investors would rather jump off a pier than risk their money trading futures. Futures have the reputation of being very risky and as being a financial tool used by professional traders or speculators who have a penchant for gambling. It's just not true. Futures can be an effective tool to both limit risk and maximize profits for a long-term investor.

A futures contract is a legal obligation to buy or deliver a particular asset at a specific time, at a specific place, at a specific price, and with a specific quality and quantity. The subject of futures is a complicated one; frankly I could write an entire book on the subject but in this chapter I'm going to give you a powerful primer that will hopefully give you a working understanding of futures and how to use them.

To begin let's examine several key advantages of using futures when investing or speculating in gold.

1. **Leverage:** Most futures have leverage of 20:1 to 5:1, in other words a one dollar move in the underlying asset can mean a $20 move in a futures account. If you use margin for stocks you know that the leverage is only 2:1 and that there is an interest expense to borrow on margin. There is no interest expense for leverage in the futures market.

2. **Liquidity:** The futures participants include professionals, hedgers, speculators, and international investors. Many futures markets have many participants and this aids in better liquidity and efficiency in prices. It's better to have thousands of buyers

and sellers than a handful. The buy and sell spread will be smaller and prices should be less volatile.

3. **Market Intelligence:** Commitment of Traders Reports (COT) published in some financial papers let you know what the professional and commercial traders are doing. Studies indicate that commercial hedgers as a group tend to get correct market turns better than other participants for most commodities, although the COT data for each market have their own personality and require independent analysis. You normally do not want to go against the commercial traders. Individual traders and speculators tend to be wrong about the market turns. Many traders use the individual trader as a contrarian indicator.

4. **No directional bias:** Most assets allow you to make money only if the asset is increasing in value. You can make money using futures in declining or rising markets. The structure of futures markets makes it quick and easy to go long in rising markets or to go short in declining markets.

5. **Excellent vehicle for hedging:** This allows a seller to lock in today's price for future delivery and it allows a buyer to lock in today's price for future delivery

6. **Cash-efficient way to trade:** Futures accounts use daily marking to market. Briefly, marking to market allows immediate access to gains and also can keep losses manageable.

Despite the clear advantages of futures, I would be remiss not to cover the *disadvantages* of the futures market:

1. **You could lose more than your initial deposit:** We will see in our upcoming examples that you can lose more than your initial deposit. This is a major drawback of futures. Risk management and a high risk tolerance are needed for the futures market.

2. **Emotional Risks:** The worst decision a speculator or investor can make is an emotional decision. Because the leverage is so high and losses and gains can be substantial,

only experienced investors should consider speculating in futures. If you are hedging, you should solicit experienced, knowledgeable, and honest help.

3. **Limit Pricing:** It can be frustrating for traders and hedgers when a market really moves and the market stops trading because of limit pricing. The market actually stops trading so you can't exit the trade until the market opens again. There is more about limit pricing for gold in the pricing section of this chapter.

4. **Inefficient hedging and pricing:** It is possible that the underlying asset and futures will not move dollar for dollar.

Hedging

I highly recommend that you always hold on to some gold, and hedging can help you do just that during gold bear markets. Remember, hedging is not meant to create a profit but to protect an asset. The commodities markets were formally established in the United States in 1848 by the Chicago Board of Trade (CBOT) to hedge price risk among farmers, food processors, and wholesalers — in other words, producers and users. There was a natural need by farmers and food processors to hedge their risks. The farmer would plant seeds and it would take several months before the crop could be harvested and brought to market. The farmer would have weather, government policy/subsidy, and competitive risks with his crops that he wanted to mitigate. The food processor had his own set of risks that he also wanted to control. The farmer wanted to lock in today's price for delivery at a future date and the food processor or wholesaler also wanted to lock in prices. The CBOT developed futures contracts to shift price risk from the farmer to the processor and vice versa. Over time speculators became participants, as they were willing to take on the price risk in anticipation of profits from potential price changes.

Each contract specifies:

1. Time

2. Quality

3. Quantity

4. Delivery location

The price is determined by the market (which is set by the buyers and sellers). The price you buy or sell at is the contract agreement.

The societal benefits of the futures market have been manifold:

1. **Abundant supplies:** As the risk of producing drops, more suppliers enter the markets and supplies increase.

2. **Better pricing:** The participants of the markets including producers, users and speculators cause the spread between the buyer and seller to be competitive, thereby creating more stable prices.

3. **Better quality:** The futures contract spells out the quality for delivery of the commodity involved. This assures the buyer of minimum standards.

4. **Price discovery:** All the participants, users, producers, and speculators determine what the price is for each commodity every day during market hours.

5. **Liquidity:** The exchanges bring together a large group of buyers, sellers, and speculators. The exchange and its clearinghouse allow for quick transactions. Once a trade is cleared, the clearinghouse will take the opposite side of each trade guaranteeing its contractual obligation.

The futures market has proliferated for every market you can imagine from soybeans to the weather. The biggest markets include energies, commodities, financials, currencies, and precious metals.

Gold Futures Contract Specifications

Gold futures are traded on the Commodity Exchange Inc. (COMEX), a subsidiary of the New York Mercantile Exchange.

Gold contracts are also traded on other exchanges around the world, most notably in London, but we'll focus on the U.S. market.

Let's look at a gold futures contract and see how it trades. Once we understand the contract specifications we can then learn how we would hedge our gold positions.

Quantity

Each contract represents 100 troy ounces. A troy ounce is the standard unit of weight for gold. One troy ounce equals 31.1034807 "grams." There are twelve troy ounces per pound as opposed to sixteen normal ounces.

Price Quotations

Prices are quoted in dollars and cents per troy ounce, for example, $350 per troy ounce.

Now we can calculate how much each contract is worth. In our example, gold is priced at $350 per ounce, so each contract is worth $35,000 (100 troy ounces * $350). If you were to buy one contract, you would have to put up a good faith deposit or initial margin requirement that you would deposit with your broker. The margin is set by the exchanges and is normally 5% to 20% of the contract value. For example if the margin were 5% you would have to deposit $1,750 ($35,000 * 5%) into your futures brokerage account for each gold contract you wish to trade.

As we mentioned, futures have tremendous price leverage; because of this the exchanges have established price limits a market can make to avoid substantial losses for participants. This price limit information is taken from the COMEX Web site for the gold market.

Initial price limit, based upon the preceding day's settlement price, is $75 per ounce. Two minutes after either of the two most active month's trades at the limit, trades in all months of futures and options will cease for a fifteen-minute period. Trading will also cease if either of the two active months is bid at the upper limit or offered at the lower limit for two minutes without trading.

Trading will not cease if the limit is reached during the final twenty minutes of a day's trading. If the limit is reached during the final half hour of trading, trading will resume no later than ten minutes before the regular closing time.

When trading resumes after a cessation of trading, the price limits will be expanded by increments of 100.

Trading Period

Contracts trade during calendar months starting with the current month and during the next two calendar months. Trading terminates at the close of business on the third-to-last business day of the maturing delivery month.

Delivery

Most futures participants do not take actual delivery or deliver gold. Less than 2% of contracts are delivered. Most traders will enter into an offsetting position. We will discuss offsetting positions in one of our examples.

In the rare case that the contract is held to expiration for delivery, the gold delivered against the futures contract must bear a serial number and identifying stamp of a refiner approved and listed by the exchange. Delivery must be made from a depository located in the Borough of Manhattan, New York City, licensed by the exchange.

Grade and Quality Specifications

The seller must deliver 100 troy ounces (±5%) of refined gold, assaying not less than .995 fineness, cast either in one bar or in three one-kilogram bars, and bearing a serial number and identifying stamp of a refiner approved and listed by the exchange.

Futures Pricing

The price of the contract is not set by specifications of the exchanges but by the markets. It is the buyers and sellers who set the price.

	Last	Open High	Open Low	High	Low	Most Recent Settle	Change	Open Interest
June 2003	349.3	0.0	0.0	0.0	0.0	349.3	0.0	0
July 2003	346.0	0.0	0.0	0.0	0.0	346.0	0.0	1
August 2003	346.3	346.0	345.7	348.1	344.5	346.3	0.0	102067
September 2003	346.7	0.0	0.0	0.0	0.0	346.7	0.0	0
October 2003	347.4	0.0	0.0	348.6	345.9	347.0	0.4	8669
December 2003	347.7	0.0	346.8	349.5	345.5	347.6	0.1	26856
February 2004	348.3	0.0	0.0	348.3	346.3	348.1	0.2	10431
April 2004	348.6	0.0	0.0	0.0	0.0	348.6	0.0	4279
June 2004	349.1	0.0	0.0	0.0	0.0	349.1	0.0	10097
August 2004	349.6	0.0	0.0	0.0	0.0	349.6	0.0	560
October 2004	350.1	0.0	0.0	0.0	0.0	350.1	0.0	224
December 2004	352.0	0.0	0.0	352.0	352.0	350.7	1.3	13200
February 2005	351.3	0.0	0.0	0.0	0.0	351.3	0.0	1324

Figure 15.1: Gold Futures Price Table from the COMEX

Notice the circled section in Figure 15.1. These are the closing prices for gold futures contract for a specific day. The nearest contract month price is very close to the gold cash price. Notice each month's price is slightly higher after July. Each month the price has to reflect the *cost to carry*. The cost to carry includes interest cost, insurance, and storing costs. As each month gets closer to expiration the cost to carry is reduced.

Margin on Futures Accounts

Trading in futures may only be done in a margin futures account. The broker who handles futures must have a Series 3

Commodities Broker's License. Most stockbrokers do not have a Series 3, and likewise most Series 3 Commodities Brokers do not have a stockbroker's license. There are many firms that specialize in futures; you can find them on the Web using a search engine.

Margin is the amount of equity that must be deposited when a futures position, either long or short, is initiated. When a position is started, a margin deposit is required immediately. This margin is called the initial margin. The initial margin can be met with cash or securities. Many exchanges allow 80% of the market value of U.S. Treasuries having a maturity of greater than three years to be used as margin.

The minimum amount that must be maintained in the account is called *maintenance margin.* If the account drops below the minimum level, then a maintenance call will be made for an additional deposit called variation margin. The maintenance margin levels vary and are generally around 20 % to 25% below the initial margin levels. The account must be brought back to the minimum requirement level immediately, normally within 24 hours, or the asset will be sold just like with stocks bought on margin.

Let's look at how the initial and maintenance margins work. Let's say the initial margin is $1,000 and maintenance margin is $800. As long as the equity position in the account remains above $800 no additional deposits will be required. Once the equity falls below $800, let's say to $750, a variation call would be sent out mandating a $250 deposit immediately to bring the account back to $1,000, the initial minimum requirement.

Hedging Example

Let's think about how you would hedge your gold position. Assume you have a portfolio of gold worth $200,000. Prices have hit your target of $1,000; you want to keep your gold but you would like to hedge at these prices.

You would need two contracts to hedge your $200,000 gold positions. Each contract is worth $100,000 (100 troy ounces, one contract ∗ $1,000 price of gold). Two contracts would be worth $200,000. Let's assume that the exchange margin requirement is still 5%; hence you would have to deposit $10,000 ($200,000 ∗ 5%) into your brokerage account.

You would probably sell a one- or two-month contract. If the price is still falling in two months you could always roll down to another month out and keep rolling down until the downtrend is over.

You would sell, or "short," two contracts of gold futures, locking in a price of $1,000; you would have to deposit $10,000 into your commodities brokerage account. If the price of gold were to drop, it could drop rather sharply and quickly. Let's assume prices drop to $700. Because you sold the two contracts when prices were $1,000, you essentially locked in a price of $1,000.

You could deliver your gold, as you had sold it at $1,000 and you would receive $200,000 in your account, even though at $700 your gold portfolio would be worth $140,000 before delivery. This is assuming that the gold you own is in deliverable form.

We want to hold on to the gold portfolio, so we could lift the hedge by placing a buy order, which would give us a profit of $60,000. The easiest way to calculate your gains or losses is to take the net change of the futures contract and multiply it by the number of units in the contract.

In this example that would be $1000 − $700 ∗ 200 troy ounces = $60,000. We will have a profit on the futures that is equivalent to the loss on the gold portfolio.

If prices rise you will lose on the futures side but the gold will appreciate. Let's use an example where prices move up using the same contracts:

Sell two August gold contracts and deposit $10,000.

Now let's say the price of gold moves up 10%.

The futures value would be $220,000 ($1,100 price of gold ∗ 2 ∗ 100).

You sold for a value of $200,000.

Gold indicators suggest gold can continue higher and you decide to exit the position. You would have to buy back the contracts at a loss. $1,000 – 1,100 = – $100 * 200 (2 contracts) The loss would be $20,000. Your initial $10,000 would be wiped out and you would have to bring in another $10,000.

Your gold would be worth 10% more, so it is a wash at this point. In reality this is not how the trade would work. Because futures are highly leveraged positions they are marked to market every day, and the account must always contain the minimum equity. If not, a maintenance call is initiated.

Let's use an example of how margin calls work. Remember that the original margin deposited was $10,000, 5% of the two contracts for gold at $1,000. Let's also assume that 80% of the equity, or $8,000, must be maintained. Make sure you understand what the initial and maintenance requirements are when you place your trades as they can and do change. Let's say the price jumped to $1,020 per ounce. Your loss would be $4,000 ($1,000 sold – $1,020 current price * 200 troy ounces) leaving an equity of $6,000. A margin call would go out for $4,000 to bring the account back to the original margin of $10,000. Now we can see why futures accounts are marked to market every day so that cash losses do not stack up against positions.

Gold Futures Speculating

Speculators are attracted to futures because of the tremendous leverage. Speculators can control a lot of assets with a small amount of capital. In the case of gold, you can control 100 troy ounces of gold with 5% initial margin of the asset value.

Let's review our previous hedging example: The price of gold is $350, so the value of one futures contract is $35,000 (100 troy ounces * $350). The speculator is required to deposit 5% of the value of the contract which is $1,750 ($35,000 * 5%).

If the price of gold moves up $1 the contract increases $100 in value ($1 increase * 100 troy ounces) and our percentage move is 5.7% (100 /$1,750).

Let's look at how we would leverage the opportunity of gold with futures, especially with my forecast for gold at $1,000.

	Last	Open High	Open Low	High	Low	Most Recent Settle	Change	Open Interest
June 2003	349.3	0.0	0.0	0.0	0.0	349.3	0.0	0
July 2003	346.0	0.0	0.0	0.0	0.0	346.0	0.0	1
August 2003	346.3	346.0	345.7	348.1	344.5	346.3	0.0	102067
September 2003	346.7	0.0	0.0	0.0	0.0	346.7	0.0	0
October 2003	347.4	0.0	0.0	348.6	345.9	347.0	0.4	8669
December 2003	347.7	0.0	346.8	349.5	345.5	347.6	0.1	26856
February 2004	348.3	0.0	0.0	348.3	346.3	348.1	0.2	10431
April 2004	348.6	0.0	0.0	0.0	0.0	348.6	0.0	4279
June 2004	349.1	0.0	0.0	0.0	0.0	349.1	0.0	10097
August 2004	349.6	0.0	0.0	0.0	0.0	349.6	0.0	560
October 2004	350.1	0.0	0.0	0.0	0.0	350.1	0.0	224
December 2004	352.0	0.0	0.0	352.0	352.0	350.7	1.3	13200
February 2005	351.3	0.0	0.0	0.0	0.0	351.3	0.0	1324

Figure 15.2: Gold Futures Price Table

A speculator can choose between buying a near contract or going out to a year and a half. The February 2005 has a cost to carry of approximately 1.5%, so we do not want to pay for that. We could go in the middle where the cost to carry is less, but we may wind up with more commission costs.

Bill Johnson, our resident futures guru, explains an excellent strategy called rollups for long-term plays such as gold and our target price of $1,000. Bill Johnson explains this strategy in his book, **Power Hedging,** and in his options seminars. Basically the strategy is based on how to play a long-term forecast by purchasing the short-term months. This allows you to roll up your position to the next month at a higher price, while taking profits and maintaining a position. I will go over the first few steps to help you understand the idea behind the strategy.

Step 1

We will purchase five August contracts at $346.30, which would cost us $8,657.50 (500 troy ounces * $346.30 * 5%). There is plenty of open interest and liquidity with this contract.

The last column of Figure 15.2 lists open interest, an important factor to consider when entering a position. Open interest is the total amount of long positions *or* short positions. It is not the *total* number of short *and* long positions. Counting the longs and shorts would be double counting, because with each short there is a long and vice versa.

Compare low open interest to a roach motel: You can get in, but you can't get out.

Look at the October 2004 contract (Figure 15.2) and notice it has the lowest open interest, 224 contracts. That is probably still enough open interest, but you would not want to own more than twenty contracts, which would be about 10% of the open interest. The August contract has the largest open interest, 102,067 contracts. Bid and ask spreads are normally better on the large open interest contracts. Make sure the month you select has plenty of contracts, otherwise known as liquidity.

Three months later the price of gold falls to $335. A margin call would be initiated.

The margin call would be for $5,650 ($346.3 – 335 * 500). You would have to deposit $5,650 to bring the account up to its initial margin of $8,657.50. Total deposit would now be $14,307.50 ($8,657.50 + $5,650). Most futures veterans will use stop orders and other risk management tools to minimize the risk with futures.

Let's suppose that by May gold is $525. The profits would be $89,350 ($525 – $346.30 * 500 troy ounces) on a $14,307.50 investment/deposit, a 624% return.

If we would have bought an equivalent amount of gold, then the net dollar amount we would have made would be $14,307.50/$345 * 1 troy ounces = approximately 41 ounces. If gold increased to

$525 then the physical gold would generate a profit of $7,257. 41 *
$177 ($525 – $348). Again, that would be a profit of $7,257 for the
physical gold and $89,350 for the gold futures contracts.

Step 2

Using the rollup strategy, we would now buy five contracts at current prices and pocket the rest as a profit. Let's say gold is now trading between $500 and $525 so we enter an order to buy five contracts
at $500. We deposit $12,500 (500 troy ounces * $500 * 5%) when
the order is executed at $500. We would pocket $76,850 ($89,350
profit from previous five contracts minus $12,500 deposit for new
five contracts) as a profit and still maintain five contracts in gold.

There would probably be at least one maintenance requirement,
so let's say total deposits are now $17,000 but gold eventually rises
to $700. Our profit for this set of contracts is $100,000 ($700 sold
– $500 bought * 500 troy ounces) with a deposit of $17,000. Our
gains would be $189,350 with a $17,000 deposit.

We are still not at our price target of $1,000, so we would roll up
again by buying five new contracts and pocketing the rest of the profit. It should be apparent that if you want to speculate and you have
the risk tolerance and capital, futures can provide huge returns.

There are options on futures that trade on the futures exchanges
that should not be confused with options that trade on options
exchanges. Do not confuse the two. Options on futures are beyond
the scope of this book; however, the next chapter will examine
hedging and speculating with options on the options exchanges.

Chapter 16
Hedging and Speculating with Gold Index Options

For the purpose of understanding options, forget about everything you've learned about futures, since futures are essentially the underlying asset leveraged with time expiration. Options are a bit more complicated. Let's go over the very basics of options with examples of how you can use options to hedge or speculate. I would like to refer to our options education Web site where we have an excellent free online course on options and options analytic tools.

Here is the Web site address:

www.21stcenturyoptionseducation.com

Options tend to be a favorite vehicle for speculating, but like futures they were originally introduced as a hedging tool.

Advantages and Disadvantages of Options

Advantages

1. **Low cost:** Options are usually inexpensive. If you are *buying* options there are no margin or maintenance calls. Selling options uncovered and using other advanced strategies will require margin and maintenance calls.

2. **Bi-directional:** Options can provide returns in rising *and* falling markets.

3. **Leverage:** A small amount of capital can control a large asset.

4. **Flexibility:** You can use options to hedge and/or speculate. Options offer conservative and aggressive strategies. There

are also options strategies to help you reduce your investment costs and even to produce income. They are excellent compliments to your overall portfolio when used properly.

Disadvantages

1. **Time decay:** The biggest disadvantage of options is time decay. Options can be frustrating for a novice; he may be right about the direction but if he picks the wrong option he can still lose money because of time decay.

2. **Complicated:** Options are more difficult to master than other assets. To have sustained success in options, one must possess knowledge, experience and discipline. Most options experts suggest learning a system that works for you and sticking to that system.

3. **Bid-ask spreads:** Many option participants complain about large spreads, the difference between the bid and ask. This difference can add 10% to 20% to your trading costs.

4. **High commissions:** Most brokers charge more commissions for options than for other transactions. Options do require more hand-holding, guidance and monitoring than other assets.

5. **Risk:** Options can be speculative and risky; you should only use risk capital if you're speculating. Sometimes novices in options get lucky with the first couple of trades they try. This is the worst learning experience you can have. This often leads to overconfidence and a false belief that options are easy. What normally follows is the trader becomes more confident and aggressive and he winds up losing not only his risk capital but also some of his investment capital. This is the same phenomenon that explains why there are ATMs inside of casinos.

Options

At the time of this writing, there is not a good way to hedge physical gold with gold options. The options available are gold stock indexes, which are better for hedging a portfolio of gold stocks.

Futures are legal obligations, whereas options are rights; you have the *right* to buy or sell but not the *obligation* to buy or sell.

Before selecting an appropriate option, you must answer the following questions.

1. Are prices likely to go up or down and why?

2. What is the price target and why?

3. When will it happen and why?

You should be able to say, prices are moving up/down to my price target within a certain time frame because if you can answer these questions your chances for success are greater. This is true for all investing and trading. There is no way to answer the above questions with certainty, but you must have a sense of the market and the stock index you are interested in before you select an option.

Options have several components that you need to become familiar with before you begin hedging or speculating. Table 16.1 is an options table, also called an options chain, which most online services will display. It lists the main components of an option.

GOX-E (CBOE)
Jul 01,2003 @ 12:13 ET (Data 15 Minutes Delayed)

Calls	Last Sale	Net	Bid	Ask	Vol	Open Int
03 Jul 50.00 (GOX GJ-E)	0	pc	16.20	17.00	0	0
03 Jul 55.00 (GOX GK-E)	0	pc	11.30	12.10	0	0
03 Jul 60.00 (GOX GL-E)	5.00	pc	6.60	7.10	0	28
03 Jul 65.00 (GOX GM-E)	1.80	pc	2.70	3.10	0	29
03 Jul 70.00 (GOX GN-E)	0	pc	0.65	0.90	0	0
03 Aug 50.00 (GOX HJ-E)	0	pc	16.30	17.10	0	0
03 Aug 55.00 (GOX HK-E)	0	pc	11.50	12.30	0	0
03 Aug 60.00 (GOX HL-E)	0	pc	7.30	7.80	0	0
03 Aug 65.00 (GOX HM-E)	0	pc	3.90	4.30	0	0
03 Aug 70.00 (GOX HN-E)	0	pc	1.80	2.05	0	0
03 Sep 50.00 (GOX IJ-E)	15.70	pc	16.30	17.10	0	13
03 Sep 55.00 (GOX IK-E)	11.60	pc	11.70	12.50	0	5
03 Sep 60.00 (GOX IL-E)	9.40	pc	7.90	8.40	0	42
03 Sep 65.00 (GOX IM-E)	6.00	pc	4.80	5.20	0	20
03 Sep 70.00 (GOX IN-E)	2.30	pc	2.60	3.00	0	18

Table 16.1: Gold Index Options Chain, CBOE Gold Index. GOX Close is $67

The Chicago Board Options Exchange's (CBOE) Gold Index (GOX) is is an equal-weighted index and reflects changes in the prices of the component stocks relative to the index base date, December 16, 1994 when the index was set to 100. The index was developed for investors and traders who wanted to hedge or speculate in gold stocks. The box index tracks the stocks in Table 16.2.

Company	Symbol
Barrick Gold	ABX
Anglogold Ltd	AU
Glamis Gold	GLG
Newmont Mining	NEM
Agnico Eagle	AEM
Fprt McMRn Cppr & Gld	FCX
Meridian Gold	MDG
Placer Dome Inc.	PDG
Ashanti Gold	ASL
Gold Fields Ltd.	GFI

Table 16.2: Components of Gold Index, GOX

Another well-known index is the XAU, the Philadelphia Gold and Silver Index. We'll discuss the XAU later in this chapter.

Calls

Table 16.1 lists all the *calls* available for the GOX in mid-year 2003 when the index was priced at $67. Calls are the option to buy the underlying asset at a specified price known as the *strike price*. You buy a call option if you think the asset is moving up enough to exceed the strike price. The call buyer has the right, but not the obligation, to buy the stock or index at a specified price for a given period of time. If you bought the July $60 calls you would have the right to buy the index at $60 at expiration. If the index closes at $80 at expiration the calls would be in a nice profit position. We will use several examples of how options work later in the chapter.

Symbols

Right below the "Calls" column are the calls available for the GOX. Each call is identified by its symbol. The first call listed is the 03 July 50. The symbol is GOXGJ.

Options symbols include the stock/index symbol, the month and the exercise price.

GOX	G	J
Gold Index	Symbol	July Expiration Exercise Price

Strike Price (Exercise Price)

Options give you the right to buy and sell stock at specified prices called strike prices. It is the buy price you are locked into through option expiration. Strikes are normally available in $5 increments for stocks/indexes above $25. Table 16.1 displays strike prices when the GOX price was $67. The strike prices available for the Gold Index were $50, $55, $60, $65, $70.

Option Expiration Cycle

Most options will trade a current month, the following month and an additional two months of the stock/index cycle. Each stock/index will be put on an option cycle for January, April, or February. There are also options available with expirations in July, August, September and December.

The CBOE Gold Index can only be exercised the day before expiration.

Expiration Dates

One of the most comprehensive aspects of options is that they expire and are thus known as wasting assets. Options values can decline solely from the passage of time.

Trading in GOX options will ordinarily cease on the business day (usually a Thursday) preceding the day on which the exercise-settlement value is calculated. Technically, options expire on the Saturday following the third Friday of the month.

Like futures, most options are not exercised by the option holder actually taking delivery of the underlying stock or index. Most are settled for cash or expire worthless.

Let's look at an example of three options at expiration when the GOX is at $67, unchanged from the price of the close for the above option chain.

1. If you bought the July $60 strike price calls you would pay the asking price of $7.10. Again, you have paid $7.10 for the option to buy the GOX at $60 by July, roughly one month from the time of purchase. The July GOX $60 calls are called *deep-in-the-money* options. If the index price is unchanged at expiration the option will still have a value of $7. The value at expiration would be the price at expiration minus the strike price would be $7 ($67 – $60). The option would lose 10 cents of its original purchase. The option is said to close with *intrinsic value.* If the GOX was at exactly $67 on expiration day, then this option would wind up with a slight loss.

   You could close the position before the market close; you would have to sell at the bid price which would be slightly lower. If you don't close out the position then the gold index is settled in cash, settlement value minus exercise. Letting it expire and settle in cash when the option is *in-the-money* will normally be the best course of action because you will avoid a commission on the sell and you will not have to sell at the bid.

   You do not have to hold the option to expiration; you can sell them at any time. While the markets are open the option will be priced. We discuss how options are priced later in this chapter.

2. The July $65 calls would cost $3.10, the asking price. If the price closed at $67 at expiration, the intrinsic value of the option would be $2 ($67 index price minus $65 exercise price). The loss on the option would be about $110 ($3.1 the cost of option minus $2, the value of option at expiration) plus commission.

3. The July $70 calls would cost 90 cents, the asking price. These are called *out-of-the-money* options. If the index prices closed at $67 the option would expire worthless. No one would pay for the privilege of settling a $70 option when the price is $67 and when there is no time left.

Generally, for novices it is better to buy deep in the money options as they act more like the stock or index and move nearly dollar-for-dollar. There are strategies and times when you would buy out-of-the-money options, but these strategies are beyond the scope of this book.

Option Price

The next four columns in Table 16.1 contain the price of the options, the last price, price change ("pc" is the price close), the bid and ask. These quotes are similar to how stocks are quoted except the bid and ask spread for these options is rather wide.

The options price is also known as the premium and it is has two different components: *intrinsic value* and *time value*. Intrinsic value is defined as the difference between the index/stock price and the exercise price (stock/index price minus exercise price) for calls. If the number is positive, the option has intrinsic value; if zero or negative, the option has only time value.

If we look at the GOX July 50, GOXGJ, the price is $17. The intrinsic value is $17 ($67, the index price minus $50, the exercise price). We would say that the option is "$17 in the money" and it has intrinsic value.

A multiplier of 100 is used with these index options. The total cost of the options would be $1,700 ($17 price for July 50 options * 100) plus commission.

The time value is the premium minus the intrinsic value. This option has no time premium; time value would be $0 ($17 – $17). At expiration the July 50 would be worth $17, its intrinsic value, at expiration if the price remained at $67.

Let's look at another example:

The GOX July 70 is selling for 90 cents or $90 (90 cents, the price of the option * 100, for one contract).

$67 – $70 (index price – exercise price) = –3. This means the option's value is pure time premium; there is no intrinsic value, so if the price stays the same at expiration the option will expire worthless.

There are basically five variables that determine the price of an option:

1. **Price:** The price of the underlying option. The higher the price of the stock/index the more expensive the option will be priced.

2. **Time:** The longer the option has until expiration the more expensive the option.

3. **Strike Price:** The further the strike price is below the price of the underlying asset the more expensive the option will be. For example, if a stock is $30, a $25 exercise option will be more expensive than a $35 option.

4. **Interest Rates:** If rates are high, calls will be comparatively more expensive and puts will be less expensive; when rates are low calls will be less expensive and puts will be more expensive.

5. **Volatility:** Volatility is the most important factor that determines an options price. Volatility is the relative tendency for the stock or index to make large up and down price swings.

The higher the volatility of a given index or of a period in the market, the more expensive the option will be.

Size of Contracts

One option contract contains 100 shares. There are exceptions for stock splits, stocks that are merging and other adjustments made by the companies. The cost to buy a contract is 100 * the option price. For example, if the price of the IBM options is $5, then the price you pay for one contract is $500 (100 shares * $5 price of option) plus commission. You can buy or sell contracts in whole numbers only.

Volume and Open Interest

The last two columns of Table 16.1 are the *volume* and *open interest* for each options series for this particular index. Volume is the number of contracts that changed hands for that day. The open interest tells us how many contracts exist — the net of long and short positions. If a trader "buys to open" and another "sells to open" then open interest will increase by the number of contracts involved because both trades are opening. If the orders are "buy to open" and the other "sell to close" then the open interest will remain unchanged. If both the buy and sell are closed then open interest will decrease by the amount of contracts involved.

Open interest is the liquidity of the contract and is an important consideration. Remember the "roach motel" where you can check in but you can't check out. If you were to buy only five contracts of the July $60 calls, you would own more than 10% (5/28) of the contracts. You can still make money in low open interest options but novices should stick to higher open interest contracts.

The open interest numbers are low for the GOX Index, meaning that liquidity is limited. Let's look at other gold indexes that have higher liquidity and open interest.

The Gold and Silver Index (XAU)

The Gold and Silver Index (XAU) is a very popular index for gold. As the name implies it is not the ideal vehicle to hedge a pure gold portfolio, but the options based on this index normally do have greater liquidity. Table 16.3 lists the stocks that make up the index, and Table 16.4 shows an options chain for the index.

Company	Symbol
Barrick Gold	ABX
Frprt-MCM	FCX
Harmony Gold Mining	HMY
Placer Dome	PDG
Agninco Eagle	AEM
Gold Fields Ltd	GFI
Meridian Gold	MDG
Apex Silver Mines	SIL
Anglogold Ltd	AU
Gold Corp	GG
Newmont Mining	NEM

Table 16.3: Components of Gold and Silver Index (XAU)

Puts	Last Sale	Net	Bid	Ask	Vol	Open Int
03 Jul 40.00 (XAU SH-X)	0	pc	0	0.30	0	0
03 Jul 45.00 (XAU SI-X)	0	pc	0	0.30	0	0
03 Jul 50.00 (XAU SJ-X)	0	pc	0	0.20	0	0
03 Jul 55.00 (XAU SK-X)	0.05	pc	0	0.25	0	105
03 Jul 60.00 (XAU SL-X)	0.05	pc	0	0.05	0	141
03 Jul 65.00 (XAU SM-X)	0.05	pc	0	0.30	0	385
03 Jul 70.00 (XAU SN-X)	0.15	pc	0	0.30	0	2009
03 Jul 75.00 (XAU SO-X)	0.30	--	0.25	0.30	15	1838
03 Jul 80.00 (XAU SP-X)	1.75	+0.20	1.65	1.95	224	1658
03 Jul 85.00 (XAU SQ-X)	9.00	pc	5.20	5.90	0	53
03 Jul 90.00 (XAU SR-X)	12.30	pc	9.90	10.60	0	57
03 Jul 95.00 (XAU SS-X)	0	pc	14.70	15.70	0	0
03 Jul 100.0 (XAV ST-X)	19.50	pc	19.70	20.70	0	2
03 Sep 50.00 (XAU UJ-X)	0.10	pc	0	0.30	0	396
03 Sep 55.00 (XAU UK-X)	0.25	pc	0	0.30	0	9363
03 Sep 60.00 (XAU UL-X)	0.30	pc	0.05	0.35	0	441
03 Sep 65.00 (XAU UM-X)	0.60	pc	0.45	0.75	0	1562
03 Sep 70.00 (XAU UN-X)	1.15	pc	1.05	1.55	0	578
03 Sep 75.00 (XAU UO-X)	2.65	pc	2.75	3.10	0	1377
03 Sep 80.00 (XAU UP-X)	4.90	-2.10	4.80	5.40	1	151
03 Sep 85.00 (XAU UQ-X)	10.20	pc	7.90	8.60	0	225

Table 16.4: Option Chain for Gold and Silver Index, XAU

Hedging with Options

Puts

The options chain in Table 16.4 is a list of XAU puts. *Puts* give the option owner the right but not the obligation to sell an asset for the strike price within a given time. For example, if you bought the August $80 puts you would have the right to sell your index for $80. If the index falls to $60 you would have a buyer at $80, so you would have locked in a price for yourself.

A way to remember the difference between puts and calls is you "call up," and you "put down." You buy calls if you think the asset will go up, and you buy a put if you think the asset will go down.

For this example, let's say we want to hedge our portfolio from falling prices, so we will buy puts. Let's say our hedge is for a

$100,000 gold stock portfolio. We can see that that this index has much more liquidity than the GOX.

Here is what we should be looking for when selecting an option for hedging:

1. **Timing:** We want to buy a short-term option no more than two months out. Remember we can roll down if the trend continues down.

2. **Strike price:** We want it to be deep in the money, as this will follow the index the closest, almost dollar for dollar. In this optimistic example, we'll have to assume that the index has tripled to around $240.

3. **Quantity:** We have $100,000 worth of gold stocks and we want to hedge because gold has moved from $350 to our target of $1,000.

4. **Liquidity:** Make sure that the contracts you purchase are no more than 5% of the open interest.

We want to buy puts to protect ourselves against falling prices. If prices fall 30%, we need to protect our portfolio for about $30,000, or about five contracts of two-month deep-in-the-money $250 puts. Remember we are assuming the XAU is at $240 and we want deep-in-the-money puts. There are many option calculators on the Web that can help you calculate the theoretical value of an option. The theoretical values are normally very close to the values at which the options would actually trade in the market. Here is the CBOE Web site which offers option tools and an options calculator:

www.cboe.com/LearnCenter/OptionsToolbox.asp

The options calculator is giving this option, a two-month $250 XAU put, a theoretical value of $14.93. This option is $10 points in the money so we are paying $4.93 for time premium. Think of the $4.93 as insurance. We would need five contracts costing $7,465 ($14.93 for a two-month $250 XAU put * 500 [five contracts]).

If the index falls 30% to approximately $168 our options should move almost dollar-for-dollar. Our profit for the option would be $33,535 ($250 – 168 ∗ 5 contracts – $7,465 cost of protective puts). Theoretically we have hedged our portfolio with the profit from the options. We have seen that stock prices tend to fall more than actual gold, so some puts should be held for insurance in case gold stock prices fall more.

If prices move up, you will probably lose the time premium, $4.93 per contract, as the rise in prices of the portfolio will be offset with the fall of the options price.

Speculating

Remember that when you speculate with futures or options, you should only use risk capital. Again if you're a novice to options buy near-term options that are deep in the money because they will move almost dollar-for-dollar to the underlying asset.

Rollup strategies work very well with options. Let's use this example:

The Gold and Silver Index (XAU) is $79.81. The option we select should fit the following parameters.

1. Call: We think prices are going up

2. Deep-in-the-money-call

3. One- to two-month option

4. Liquidity: You don't want more than 5% of the open interest.

XAU-X (Philadelphia)   **79.81**   -0.89

Jul 06,2003 @ 11:43 ET (Data 20 Minutes Delayed)   **Bid** 0 **Ask** 0 **Size** 0x0 **Vol** 0

Calls	Last Sale	Net	Bid	Ask	Vol	Open Int
03 Jul 65.00 (XAU GM-X)	15.50	pc	14.30	15.30	0	336
03 Jul 70.00 (XAU GN-X)	9.80	-0.90	9.50	9.80	205	529
03 Jul 75.00 (XAU GO-X)	5.20	-1.00	4.90	5.50	22	1705
03 Jul 80.00 (XAU GP-X)	1.80	-0.30	1.50	1.80	334	5326
03 Jul 85.00 (XAU GQ-X)	0.30	-0.05	0.15	0.45	172	3618
03 Jul 90.00 (XAU GR-X)	0.20	pc	0.05	0.30	0	254
03 Jul 95.00 (XAU GS-X)	0.30	pc	0	0.15	0	6
03 Jul 100.0 (XAV GT-X)	0	pc	0	0.15	0	0
03 Aug 40.00 (XAU HH-X)	0	pc	39.30	40.30	0	0
03 Aug 45.00 (XAU HI-X)	0	pc	34.40	35.40	0	0
03 Aug 50.00 (XAU HJ-X)	0	pc	29.40	30.40	0	0
03 Aug 55.00 (XAU HK-X)	0	pc	24.40	25.40	0	0
03 Aug 60.00 (XAU HL-X)	17.00	pc	19.40	20.40	0	10
03 Aug 65.00 (XAU HM-X)	12.40	pc	14.50	15.50	0	40
03 Aug 70.00 (XAU HN-X)	11.20	pc	10.00	11.00	0	545
03 Aug 75.00 (XAU HO-X)	5.40	pc	6.00	6.70	0	688

Table 16.5: XAU Options Chain

The July 70 calls fit our parameters. The calls would cost $9.80 per contract and would be $9.80 in the money ($79.81 price of index minus $70 strike price) and we would not have a time premium (which is very unusual). The approximate cost would be $9,800 ($9.80 ∗ 100 or one contract) plus commissions.

In the following examples let's assume we will let the options at expiration settle in cash. You will receive (in cash) the difference between the exercise price and the actual settlement price at expiration.

If the index closes unchanged at $79.81 at expiration, we can let it settle in cash and it will end up breaking even.

Notice the other strike prices for July do have time premiums. July strike prices above $80 will expire worthless if the index price stays at $79.81 or goes lower. Let's say prices drop to $75 at expiration, $4.81 below what we paid. If we let it settle in cash we would net $5.00. Now let's say prices rise to $100 at expiration. We would make approximately $3,000 ($100 minus $70 July strike price purchased * 100, one contract). The approximate return would be 30% ($3,000 profit / $9,800 cost of one contract).

Now we can roll up to the next month, keep our initial contract and book the remaining balance as a profit. We can keep rolling up until gold reaches our target of $1,000.

One of the key points in this chapter is that options can be a great complement to any portfolio, as options provide tremendous flexibility. Learn more about the advantages of options but, more importantly, use them as a portfolio-enhancing tool.

Chapter 17
Gold Investing Mistakes to Avoid

"Mistakes Are Portals of Discovery"

— *James Joyce*

Unfortunately one of the best ways to learn about investing is to make mistakes. Whenever possible, try to learn from the mistakes of others, rather than your own. Here are some gold investment mistakes to avoid. This list is compiled from mistakes that I have made and that I have seen other investors and traders make. Some of these mistakes we have discussed in other chapters in the book. Most of the mistakes mentioned here can be applied to investing in general.

1. **Investors and traders don't plan to fail — they fail to plan.** This may be a trite saying but an important one: Make sure you have a plan.

2. **Don't make emotional decisions.** This is by far the biggest mistake investors make when they invest. The emotions of fear and greed are powerful and they can cause you to make some very stupid mistakes. We have all heard that an investor should buy low and sell high. In reality this is very difficult for most people to do. I can't tell you how many times I have told investors to buy something when prices were low and they do not because they fear prices will go lower. That same person will call me up after the investment is up 50% begging to buy because he can't stand to watch it go up and he thinks he is missing out.

   One of the greatest, most helpful investing skills you can learn is to buy when people are selling at extremes and to sell when people are buying at extremes. Of course the asset must have investment merit. Jason Goefert is a writer for sentimenTrader.com, a newsletter that we feature on our *21st Century Alert* Web site (www.21stcenturyalert.com), and he uses a catch phrase that most investors and traders should put into practice: "Make emotion work for you and not against you."

3. **Don't try to pick a top or a bottom.** Many traders and investors miss important moves because they try to pick a bottom or top. To make money you have to pick the *trend* and *direction* to make money, not the exact top or bottom.

4. **Don't be afraid to ask for advice.** Seek advice whether you're a novice or an experienced investor/trader. If you're a novice, make *sure* you seek investment advice, either from newsletters, books, Web sites or professionals. Often, seasoned professionals will ask me for advice because they are wisely seeking second opinions and objective, intelligent and honest advice.

5. **If you do seek advice, learn as much as you can about that person.** This also is true with the broker or dealer from whom you buy. It's amazing how investors will take advice from someone in an investor chat room, a person they don't know anything about, including his experience, education, background — someone they have never met. It is impossible to know if he has a conflict of interest.

6. **Analysis leads to paralysis syndrome.** It is common for new investors to spend so much time researching that they can't seem to pull the trigger. Professionals call this the "analysis leads to paralysis" syndrome. Just as it is futile to pick the exact top and bottom, it is also futile to pick the perfect investment and wait for the perfect environment. Too much analysis can cause you to miss opportunities.

7. **Speculate with risk capital only.** I have seen too many investment portfolios blow up because the portfolio had too many risky issues and strategies. We all like to have some high flyers in our portfolio — they can be fun and lucrative.

Just make sure you don't over allocate risky assets to your portfolio. Never risk more than you can afford to lose, especially with speculative option and future strategies.

8. **Don't make too small of an allocation to gold.** One of the most common mistakes I see investors make is they allocate too small a portion of their portfolio to hedging and non-related assets. Make sure you allocate enough to make a difference in your portfolio. Consider allocating at least 10% to 30% of your portfolio to gold.

9. **Diversify.** Investors who did not diversify enough in the early 2000s have certainly paid the price. A good way to enhance your returns and reduce your risk is to add non-related assets to your portfolio. Gold is an excellent complement to most stock portfolios.

10. **Never buy a gold penny stock, low capitalization, or exploration stock as a gold play.** Their fortunes are based more on the company's success, exploration efforts, and management or other factors that are more important than the price of gold.

11. **Look before you leap.** Peter Lynch, the great investment manager, mentions in his book *One Up On Wall Street* that investors spend more time researching a refrigerator they are going to buy than the stocks in which they invest. Don't make this mistake. Do your homework.

12. **If you are uncomfortable or can't get important questions answered, then don't buy.** I am often asked about "this or that" investment or broker. I will do my due diligence and find out there is very little information on the investment or broker. If you don't have the answers you need to make an informed decision then don't make the decision. When in doubt stay out. There will always be more opportunities in the future.

13. **Don't constantly watch gold prices.** If you watch the minute-to-minute day-to-day gold price fluctuations it will drive you crazy. This is especially relevant advice because

gold only moves out of a price range about 25% of the time. The rest of the time it just fluctuates in a narrow range. You do need to monitor prices and fundamentals but not to the point where you are watching hourly or daily.

I have seen this type of compulsive behavior with some investors; it leads to emotional decisions and over-trading of their account and it does not allow them to stick with long-term profitable trades. There is a saying in investing that is very true, "money is like soap, the more you play with it the less you will have."

14. **Don't neglect your investments or positions.** The opposite of compulsive behavior is neglect. This is especially true with stocks or speculative issues. I have seen many investors forget about their positions; when they finally do look at a quarterly or annual statement they are shocked by their portfolios' losses.

15. **Make sure you stay disciplined and stick to your plan.** This could mean when you get a buy signal you buy, when you get a sell signal you sell. Don't override your discipline and talk yourself out of a sound decision.

16. **Don't make investing/trading too complicated.** We tend to want to complicate matters when we don't have to. Try to keep your investing/trading to a few simple rules, like "buy low, sell high."

17. **Learn to accept mistakes, take action and learn from them.** Many smart people have blamed their mistakes on the market, analysts, market makers, everyone except themselves. If you make a mistake, make the right decision and adjust or get out. Some of our best learning experiences originate from our mistakes.

"A man who has committed a mistake and doesn't correct it is committing another mistake."

— Confucius

Chapter 18
Conclusion

The goal of this book is to provide a solid argument that the price of gold has begun a long-term rise that will reach $1,000. I also have provided sound advice, both conservative and aggressive, on how to invest or speculate in gold. The advice comes from my knowledge, industry contacts, and my own personal experience making my first fortune in gold more than twenty years ago.

History is repeating itself. I encourage you to protect yourself from the imminent dangers that the world and the markets face, and to prosper tremendously by taking advantage of the great opportunities I see for gold in the next few years.

History of Gold

It is no wonder that gold has been a prized possession of kings, rulers, legends, governments, and dynasties. It has outlasted regimes, nations, financial systems, and generational periods. Over time it has provided prestige and has proven to be a store of value, an inflation hedge, a haven of safety, and an excellent diversification vehicle. Gold has been the ultimate investment throughout history and it will continue to be.

Many countries and individuals abandoned the gold standard, as it required too much discipline and cooperation. Many economists feel very uncomfortable that the major national economies throughout the world do not use gold as their major reserve. Even though the major economies of the world are not backed by gold, this makes it even more important for individuals to have gold in their portfolio.

The Benefits of Gold

There are many benefits of gold as in investment — especially now. Here is a brief summary of the investment merits of gold:

- Gold has stood the test of time like no other investment.

- Gold has a solid track record of performance during times of world tension or inflation.

- Gold provides a variety of ways to invest or speculate.

- Liquidity: Most gold markets have deep, international participation.

- Gold is an excellent diversification asset for stock portfolio, as it is unrelated to stock performance.

- The variety of gold investment vehicles can fit into anyone's budget.

- Many books, newsletters, and Web sites are available to help investors make informed decisions about gold investments.

- Gold is followed globally, allowing investors to monitor it any time, any place.

- Gold will thrive in the current environment.

Why Gold Prices Will Rise

Many of the conditions that created the tremendous bull market in gold in the late 1970s and 1980 are reoccurring: major conflicts in the Middle East, increased money supply, uncertainty created by changing world and economic events and lackluster returns from the stock market.

History shows us there are four major conditions that cause gold prices to increase:

1. World tension

2. Financial crisis

3. Inflation

4. Supply/demand factors

We are entering a period where all four conditions will become more acute. As discussed early in the book, all these forces are developing now and will create the next great bull market in gold. The events of September 11, 2001 probably provided the biggest catalyst that changed our economy, the world, and our outlook. Many experts believe the world will experience other major terrorists attack in the next five years. We encourage you to prepare yourself and your family on a physical and financial level. Gold will be an important component of your financial future going forward.

Investment Choices

The major difference for gold investors today versus the last major gold market is the proliferation of gold investments and derivatives. Below is the ranking in terms of importance for your gold portfolio.

1. Gold coins

2. Rare gold coins

3. Gold bullion

4. Equity Gold Trust Fund *

5. Gold mutual funds

6. Individual gold stocks

7. Gold options and futures for hedging

8. Gold options and futures for speculating

---

* *Equity Gold Trust Fund is expected to start trading around June, 2004.*

Ideally you should focus on gold and rare coins and consider some hedging from time to time, especially after sharp and significant advances. Your budget, knowledge, experience, needs and goals will determine whether you should consider other gold investments

Summary

All investors have to make many important investment decisions. These decisions have to be made for any investment you make — not just gold. Let's review them:

What to buy?
Buy gold or a gold-oriented investment.

Why?
Price is going to $1,000 because of world tension, inflation, potential global financial crisis, and because demand is growing faster than slowing supply.

How much?
Gold should make up 10% to 30% of your portfolio.

When to buy?
Start now and add on pull-backs to the trend line or short-term moving average.

Monitor and adjust holdings if warranted.
Use technical and fundamental analysis to help you monitor gold and your positions.

When to sell?
Start to take profits in the $1,000 area as it pulls back to the trend line or moving averages.

With this information, you can now develop your goals and an investment plan. Make sure you implement, monitor, and stick to the plan.

Considerations for Gold Coins

- Only buy rare coins that are graded by Numismatic Guarantee Corporation (NGC) or Professional Coin Grading Service (PCGS).

- Do not buy private mint coins.

- Do not buy small units of gold bullion.

- Stick with the top five most common gold coins in the world: the American Eagle, Canadian Maple Leaf, South African Krugerrand, Australian Kangaroo, and Chinese Panda.

- Do not buy any coins that have rim nicks, scratches or abrasions.

- Do not buy any coins with carbon or copper spots.

- Do not buy "rare date" bullion coins.

- Do not buy strictly on the best price.

- Never store your gold coins in a dealer's vault; take immediate delivery.

Other investment considerations and concepts:

- Watch your costs; they can lower the return of your overall portfolio. Each category of gold mentioned will have its own set of costs. Know what the costs are before you invest.

- Have patience; it takes time for long-term trends to play themselves out.

- Trends go farther, up and down, than most people anticipate.

- Diversification is the key to an efficient portfolio. There are enhanced returns and less risk.

- Don't try to pick a bottom or top.

- Build a position; don't buy and sell all at once.

- The last phase of a major move, the frenzy stage, is characterized by a significant move up, a 90-degree ascent and lots of news coverage.

- Use all the tools you can to make decisions, like technical and/or fundamental analysis, books, newsletters, and professional advice.

- Use rollup strategies to limit risk and to participate in the upside of gold.

- Have fun learning and investing.

I live in Florida, which is famous for dramatic lightning, thunder, and rainstorms. We can tell when the storms will start; they occur during summer from three o'clock in the afternoon until six o'clock every day. The clouds billow up thousands of feet into the sky and by late afternoon they turn grey. Soon after the downpour begins, replete with lightning and thunder.

Just as I can anticipate the arrival of those storms, I can see the financial storm clouds gathering again for the markets. I never thought I would see these conditions again, but they are occurring. I have personally moved for financial cover, and this book is meant to help you see the approaching storm and to encourage you to take cover.

Gold Glossary

Alloy

A mixture of two or more metals. Gold is extremely soft, so it is often mixed with small amounts of silver or copper or other metals. The mixture of metals strengthens gold and allows the color of gold to stand out.

Ask

The price at which a person is willing to sell. The ask price normally quoted is the lowest price at which a seller is willing to sell. Also referred to as the offer. It is the price the buyer will pay since that is the price at which the seller is willing to sell.

At-the-Money

The current price is the same as the strike price of an options contract. *Example: The asset is $50 and strike price of the option is $50.*

Bid

The bid is the highest price any buyer is willing to pay. The bid is the price to which the seller would agree.

Bid-Ask Spread ("The Spread")

The difference between the bid and the ask for a contract, stock, or other asset. Normally a liquid market would have a narrow bid and ask spread and an illiquid market would have a large bid and ask spread.

Bullion

Refined bars or ingots of gold, normally of high quality. They are either stored by central banks and investors or used as raw material for industrial uses and jewelry.

Bullion Coin

A coin whose value is based on its gold content rather than any numismatic criteria. Bullion coins are minted as gold investment products and sell for a small premium above the current market price of gold.

CBOE

The Chicago Board of Options Exchange (CBOE), the world's largest options exchange.

Call Option

Gives the owner the right, but not the obligation, to buy an asset at a specified price over a given time frame. You would buy a call if you think the asset is going up in price.

Carrying Cost

The difference between the near and deferred months in a futures contract that includes storage, insurance, and interest charges.

Cash Production Cost

The cost of mining an ounce of gold incurred by such as extracting, refining, labor, and equipment.

COMEX

A subsidiary of the New York Mercantile Exchange. COMEX, Commodity Exchange Inc., is the largest and most important gold futures exchange which trades gold contracts.

Contract Month

The month in which a given futures contract becomes deliverable.

Delivery

The transfer of ownership of an asset from a seller to a buyer.

Delivery Date

The specific date when an asset must be delivered to fulfill a futures contract.

Deep-in-the-Money

When the current price is significantly above the strike price of an options contract. *Example: The current price of a stock is $50 and the strike price of a call is $40. The option in this example is $10 points deep-in-the-money.*

Double Eagle

A Unites States $20 gold coin, which was minted from 1849 through 1933. The coin is 0.900 fine and has a gold content of 0.9675 troy ounces.

Dow Theory

The basic tenets that are the foundation of technical analysis. Named for Charles Dow, who helped found the *Wall Street Journal.* The major tenet of Dow Theory is that the "market discounts everything." This sets up the basis and logic for technical analysis. It tells us to observe the market and prices to determine how investors are making decisions in the market. For example, are they bullish, pushing up prices or are they bearish and selling, pushing down prices?

Fine Gold

The purity of gold is defined in parts per 1,000. The purest form of gold is considered .9999. A gold bar of .995 fineness is 99.5 percent pure gold.

Fundamental Analysis

The study of financial statements and economic data to determine if an asset is overvalued, undervalued or fairly valued.

Futures Contract

A legally-binding agreement to buy or sell an asset. The contract generally specifies time, delivery, quantity, quality and delivery location.

Gold Leaf

Gold hammered extremely thin to be used mostly for decorative purposes.

Gold Standard

A monetary system with units of currency that can be converted into fixed amounts of gold.

Grade

The amount of a metal per metric ton of ore, usually expressed in hundredths of an ounce per ton.

Hedging

Any effort to protect a buyer or seller from financial loss. A perfect hedge is one that eliminates the possibility of a future gain or loss. It can mean buying insurance, or using futures or options. A holder of gold can sell a futures contract to hedge physical gold positions, or buy puts on a gold index to hedge a gold stock portfolio.

Initial Margin

The amount of cash or eligible securities that must be deposited in an account when a futures position is established. Also called original margin.

In-the-Money

The amount that would be received if an option was exercised immediately. A call option with a strike below, or a put option with a strike above, the current price. *Example: An asset that is currently quoting $28 and the put strike price is $30 is said to be $2 in-the-money. If the holder exercised the put, the holder could buy the asset in the market for $28 and exercise the asset for $30, profiting by $2.*

Intrinsic Value

An option's intrinsic value is the amount by which it is in-the-money.

Karat

A measure of gold's purity, fineness. 24-karat is pure gold of at least .99 fineness.

Krugerrand

Gold coin minted in South Africa since 1967, named for Paul Kruger, the last president of the Republic of South Africa. Krugerrands are 22 karat, or .9167 fine.

Leverage

The ability to control an asset with a small percentage invested for a higher return. Leverage can provide higher returns with commensurate risk.

Liquid

An active options or futures contract that has a large number of active buyers and sellers. Most investors and traders prefer liquid contracts; they tend to have better pricing and they are easier to move in and out.

Maintenance Margin

The level to which the initial margin may decrease without the client being called for additional margin.

Maple Leaf

Gold coins first minted in 1979 by Canada's Royal Canadian Mint. The Maple Leaf was the first 24-karat pure gold coin.

Margin

Futures contracts require a "good faith" deposit or performance bond where the customer deposits the required cash or eligible securities that indicates willingness and ability to perform on the contract.

Margin Call

A request sent out by a firm to a client when the margin in the account falls below the maintenance margin level. The call requires the client to immediately restore the account back to the initial margin level.

Moving Average

A technical indicator based on recent price history. A moving average can be used instead of a trend line to help determine entry and exit points for short, intermediate and long-term moves.

Numismatic Coin

A coin that is valued by investors and collectors by its rarity, aesthetics, historical significance, and other attributes besides its metal content.

Open Interest

Total net number of contracts in a futures or options market that are still open. It is an important piece of information to determine liquidity. Traders normally prefer a high open interest for an options or futures contract.

Option

The right to buy or sell an asset for a specified price within a specified period of time.

Out-of-the-Money

An option with no intrinsic value. A call option with a strike above or a put option with a strike below the current asset price. *For example, a gold index at $75 and a $80 gold index call would be $5 out-of-the money.*

Panda

First introduced in 1982, the Panda is one of the most popular gold bullion coins the world. It is a .9999 fine gold coin issued by the China Mint.

Physicals

Gold coins or bullion bars as opposed to futures contracts.

Pullback

A technical analysis term that indicates a temporary decline in prices. Prices are "pulling back" to a trend line or moving average.

Put Option

A contract that gives the holder the right, but not the obligation, to sell an asset at a specified price within a specified time period.

Rally

An upward movement in prices.

Resistance

The area on a chart where sellers overwhelm buyers and prices either consolidate or pull back. If a stock has rallied to a certain price and has been turned back repeatedly, that indicates sellers waiting there. Breaking through resistance means the sellers at that level are gone.

Scrap

Material from electronics and other items that contain gold, including jewelry, which is sent to a refiner where it is recycled. Gold mining and production is the major source of gold; scrap gold is a distant second source of gold.

Sell Short

Selling short is a way to make money if prices fall. The client borrows stock from his broker. He then sells the borrowed stock, and the sold stock shows up in his account as a credit on the cash side of his account. It shows up as a short, a negative position in the securities section in his account. If prices fall he can use the credit in his account to buy back the stock at a lower price, closing the position at a profit. If he is wrong and prices rise he will have to buy the stock at a higher price and at a loss. *Example: You sell short 100 shares of XYZ at $50. Your account will be credited with $5,000 and you will be short 100 shares of XYZ, a negative position. The stock falls to $40 and you use the credit to buy the stock back for $4,000. The stock you bought is used to cover the short and now your account is flat on the securities side. The cash side has a $1,000 profit ($5,000 sold short minus $4,000 to buy stock).*

Short Covering

The actual purchase of a security by a short seller to replace those borrowed at the time of the short sale. Short covering in a market can cause a short-term dramatic rise as traders who have shorted are covering — buying at the asked price — to either lock in a profit or minimize a loss.

Strike Price

The predetermined price at which an asset can be bought for a call or sold in the case of a put. The strike price is the same as the exercise price.

Technical Analysis

The study of prices, charts, volume and indicators to try to forecast future prices, direction, and momentum.

Time Value

The amount of an option's price that is not accounted for by intrinsic value. For example, let's say the gold index is trading for $80. You own the $85 calls and you paid $3. The call is out-of the-money and there is no intrinsic value, so the entire premium is time value.

Trend

A term in technical analysis that describes prices moving up or down. If prices are moving sideways, then prices are described as trendless or non-trending; otherwise a trend is up or down.

Trend Lines

Trend lines are used in technical analysis to help determine exit and entry points. If prices are trending up, with rising tops and bottoms, then a trend line is drawn upward by tying the bottoms of a trend with a straight line. If prices are trending down, declining tops and bottoms, then a trend line is drawn downward by tying the tops together with a straight line.

Troy Ounce

A standard unit of weight for gold. One troy ounce equals 31.1034807 grams. 32.1507 troy ounces equals one kilogram. Named after the city of Troyes, France, where the system of troy weight was first used in the fourteenth century.

Variation Margin

The amount of money that must be deposited immediately in a futures account to restore the equity back to the initial margin requirement

Volume

The number of contracts that changed hands during a given period of time, usually one trading session.

INDEX

Entries followed by *f* and *t* refer to figures and tables respectively.